TRADE, TRANSPORT AND *TANDA*

Trade, Transport and *Tanda*

SHIFTING IDENTITIES OF THE BANJARAS

MANISHA CHOUDHARY

MANOHAR
2018

First published 2018

ISBN 978-81-935609-8-3

Published by
Ajay Kumar Jain *for*
Manohar Publishers & Distributors
4753/23 Ansari Road, Daryaganj
New Delhi 110 002

Printed at
Shri Ganpati Enterprises
New Delhi 110 052

For

MA (RAMESHWARI)

&

PAPAJI (DEVI SINGH)

in Loving Memory of my Brother

'HIRA-Bunty'

on his 39th birth anniversary

(11 February 1979-18 September 2000)

Banjara ban mai phire; liye lakria haath,
Tanda waha lad gaya; jaha koi sanghi nahi saath.

The Banjara roams in the forest; with a stick in hand,
The *carvan* (troop) disintegrated and became dissolved; when no one accompanied him.

Kheti motha ri;
vyapar balda ro.

Cultivation of legume (moth: *vigna aconitifolia*);
Commerce of oxen.

Contents

Illustrations

FIGURES

MAPS

PLATES

(*at the end*)

Foreword

THE PRESENT VOLUME is based on the author's dissertation approved by the Department of History, University of Delhi. The book covers the period from thirteen to nineteenth century AD. This research is largely based on archival sources, classified and catalogued at the Rajasthan State Archives, Bikaner and extensively discusses the life and professional activities of the Banjaras, who were adroit traders and transporters. The organization of different *tandas* of the Banjaras are also discussed and analysed. The Banjaras were indispensable for state and society in medieval India. The flow of trade largely depended on the Banjaras as has been discussed by the author. The moving Banjara groups invariably came in conflict with the peasants because of the former's tendency to graze their cattle in the peasant's fields. The Banjaras also came in conflict with the local state officials on the issue of destruction of the standing crops. Needless to say that the Banjaras though indispensable for the medieval state were also occasionally a source of nuisance. The author has highlighted the vibrant role of the Banjaras during the period of the Delhi sultanate, Mughal empire, post Mughal states as well as the early phase of the colonial period. Even a casual reading of the book shows the author's clear command of the vernacular languages, especially *Dhundhari* variant of the Rajasthani language. The book also makes its own contribution in terms of research on the marginalized groups.

I will feel happy if the book acquires the popularity that it deserves. I hope Manisha Choudhary will continue the quality of research that is exuded by this work.

6 November 2017 R.P. RANA
Delhi

Acknowledgements

THIS WORK IS a revised and enlarged version of my dissertation titled 'Long Distance Trading in Mughal North-West India: Role of Banjaras', submitted at Department of History, University of Delhi in 2009. I express my deep sense of gratitude to Prof. R.P. Rana for guiding my research, offering corrective suggestions and introducing me to the treasure troves of Medieval Rajasthani Archival sources. I would like to thank my teachers namely, Prof. S.Z.H. Jafri, Prof. Amar Farooqui, Prof. R.C. Thakran, Prof. Farhat Hasan, Prof. Upinder Singh, Prof. Nayanjot Lahiri, Prof. Mahesh Rangarajan, Prof. Sunil Kumar and Dr. Prabhu Mohapatra for their valuable suggestions while I was doing my course work. My special thanks are due to Prof. Dinesh Singh for encouraging me to ferret out the original regional sources and highlighting its importance in the main history narrative. I owe a deep sense of gratitude towards Dr. Neelanjana and Prof. Anu Kapur for their constant encouragement. The contribution and long commentaries of Prof. S.N.R. Rizvi were immensely helpful as it helped to draw my attention to the etymology of *tanda.*

I am especially grateful to my parents, brothers (Sachin, Lt. Comdr. Rishi Raj and O.P. Choudhary), sister (Kiran) and sister-in-law (Monica) for encouraging me to undertake this research work and for helping me in various ways. The presence of Maira, Manu (Mira), Aditya, Abhimanyu and Vani was always refreshing and much needed. I owe special debt to my friends Dr. Mohd. Tarique Anwar, Sudhir Sharma, Dr. Shubhra Kathuria, Aadya Antya, Kavita, Mamta Sharma, R.B.A. Choudhary, Dr. Sanjeev Singh, Dr. Anju Gupta, Dr. Vijaylakshmi, Dr. Saleem Mir and Dhanesh for their varied support. The timeless long chats over unnumbered cups of tea with *Apiya* also deserve a mention here. I owe special love to Rio and Shibu. Last, but not the least I want to thank the members of the various *tandas* for the hospitality they extended to me during my visits to their *tandas.*

I would like to express my gratitude to Prof. Abha Singh (IGNOU), Mrs. Vinay Bhardwaj, and Dr. Promodini Varma who were always available whenever help was required. The role of Dr. M.A. Lari Azad and Dr. Vandana Saraswat also deserves a mention as they provided me an opportunity to bring this research into the mainstream. I am grateful to Dr. Mahendra Khadgawat, Director Rajasthan State Archives and Dr. S.P. Vyas for their encouragement to publish this research. I shall also thank the staff of Rajasthan State Archives in Bikaner, National Archives, New Delhi and Nehru Memorial Museum & Library for the assistance offered to me. A special thanks is due to Mr. Sanjiv Kumar for his hospitality and assistance at NMML.

I shall be amiss if I didnt express my heartfelt regards to the production team at Manohar who worked tirelessly and did not lose patience while I was making repeated changes in the text and it is due to their efforts that this work has attained its final shape.

Delhi MANISHA CHOUDHARY

Introduction

WRITING HISTORY INVOLVES the task of selecting a time frame. Subsequently, the theme needs to be planted firmly and elaborated, contextualizing with the main narrative. The source materials of a regional history is invariably scattered and a researcher has to navigate through various channels before arriving at a conclusion. The idea for this work came from an insight as to why the community of Banjaras have been refered in the state documents of Jaipur State so frequently? The nature of the Banjara community is that of wanderers who travelled long distance and had a large number of cattle (ox). Placing the Banjaras in Indian history helps us to understand that the huge and extensive canvas of Medieval India is incomplete without the discussion of various communities and groups, who were crucial for accomplishing various acts and events of their contemporary times. A few communities were connected to various empires directly or indirectly and were mainly guided by the economic motives or benefits to be drawn out from the many economic and political activities of the state.

The extent of historical evidence, selective archival factors, the knowledge of inscriptions, along with the idea of community and interest of historians have much to do, when the narrative of the communities and their diverse discourses are extracted out. The primary task while dealing with the history writing of communities, who maintained no written records of their own is to dig out information from diverse, often unlikely sources and local documents. Furthermore, often there are no contemporary sources to cross check the information. The consideration about the community can be made not by looking at its character in isolation but by looking at the role it played, when it co-existed, modified, negotiated and contested with the state and the local populace. In course of time some communities or groups become prominent. Further, in order to assert their presence as unique and superior from the regular populace and groups, they did innovate and developed certain cultural performances and rituals. To all these activities the previous religious associations were working as prominent historical guides and were also authenticating their backgrounds silently. The invocation of new rituals and ceremonies was an essential feature to signify the uniqueness and highlight the distinct identity of their community. Similarly, the Banjaras invoked and developed certain rituals which were facts of their day to day activities and a few were for distinguishing their groups from the various other communities of the times. 'It must be borne in mind that the discussion of community and state is not a synopsis of the history to follow, it is intended merely as a description of political context....'[1] Even today, Banjaras are maintaining their unique and distinct lifestyle and cultural activities. Similarly, one more community emerged during medieval times. The community is popularly known as that of Lohars. Lohars are also widely distinguishable due to their lifestyle (constantly on move with carts), rituals and the cultural beliefs.

There are many such groups who came to the forefront during medieval times, but these two communities are more prominently visible due to their specific endeavours and endurance. The Banjaras adopted a lifestyle of wanderers and never settled in one place. The trading and transport activities were adopted as the economic functions to sustain life and in due course of time they flourished in these activities. Not only did the Banjaras flourish, they also attained a crucial position in the trading network of the medieval times. The position of Banjaras became such that no trade activity was possible without them. They were controlling major share of trading and transport activities especially in the dry food products such as grains, salt, cotton, species, ghee, oil, etc., and various other products such as *multani*, *gond*, etc. The trading routes on which the Banjaras travelled were mainly through the forest areas and Banjaras were well versed with these unmarked routes of forests. The routes via jungle were identified by Banjaras through their indigenous techniques or innovative demarcation methods taught to the member of *tanda* while travelling through the forests. While en-route the techniques and methods of fast travel, efficient delivery (in time), identification and demarcation of forest routes were taught to the junior members of *tanda*. 'The physical setting plays a very important role in shaping the social groups.'[2] The physical settings and the environment shapes the culture, social set-up and economic activities of the region. Nature and the natural environment works like a constant definer and the respective communities get shaped accordingly. The similar kind of impact of the surrounding nature is visible on the economic and cultural activities of the Banjaras and simultaneously over a period it guided the formation of their social organization and settings. For example marriage ceremonies are organized in the month of *Sawan* (monsoon) because the trade opportunities are not available then and the *tanda* is usually halting. Whereas, the Hindu brahmanical instructions forbid marriage in the month of *Sawan*. The marriages were intra-*tanda* affair; no outsider was allowed to form matrimonial alliance with members of the *tanda*. Even today the same practice is continuing. No genetic dysfunction is visible in the *tanda* members as the *tanda* was an open entity and was constantly taking in new members whenever anyone was willing to join in as a Banjara.

The Lohar community is also very proud of their specific identity. In personal interaction with the community it was reflecting out very prominently. The Lohars take pride in the fact that they are descendants of Rana Pratap, 'the raja of Udaipur who forced Akbar to go through sleepless nights' and they say it with a strong and deep-rooted sense of pride in their ancestry. Further, they are conscious to remind a researcher again and again while describing specifications of their community, that 'we are Rajputs, Chandravanshis, who were ancestors of Raja Rana Partap of Udaipur'. This strongly reflects their sense of association with the Udaipur family. Rajputs also treat Lohars with respect, but dont fit them in the embattled identity of Rajputs.[3] Despite overwhelming claims, the Lohars manage their own affairs within community and hesitate to approach the legal system. The marriages are intra-group. The present cultural mosaic is dotted with both older and newer institutions and recognizes diverse local customary arrangements. The synthesis of religion, culture and political element lead to a product of diverse cultural heritage which is united in a classical sense of community feeling but without offering any option to bring in people from other communities. Contrary to it, the membership into the Banjara community was an open affair and anyone at choice could join the community following their own native religious and cultural practices. The free incorporation of the members from diverse cultures and communities provided a heterogeneous character to the community.

The Lohars deserted their homes and pledged not to settle into a permanent establishment till they gain victory over the Mughals. Which of course never happened. The honest part of the community lore lies in the acceptance that they were unable to defeat the Mughals. Therefore, even today in the twenty-first century they are leading a life of wanderers. The present reality of the situation is that the Mughal rule is no more surviving. It died its natural death as every other empire of the world. Does this mean that a new Mughal Empire has to be established and then defeated in order to put Lohars back into a settled lifestyle? The basic occupation undertaken by Lohars inorder to earn a livelihood is making of iron objects, mainly agricultural tools like *kus, phawara, chalna, jherr, parat, kalai, chimta, da-tali, darati*, etc.

Both the communities are identical in some of their representation specially of status through the objects and items in their possession like; both are proud about the usage of original gold and silver in their ornaments, clearly specifying 'we don't wear artificial jewellery, original gold and silver only, no artificial at all; whatever we wear it's all original' (*hum nakali gahana nahi pawai, asli sona aur chandi bas nakli katai na pawa, jo paai sache paai*). The designs of the ornaments are mainly made in Jaipuri-Jodhpuri styles. The dresses of both male and female are inspired by Rajasthani styles and designs (see Plates 5 and 7).

The wide variety and diverse reflection of these communities are driving me away from the core of this work which is the Banjara community and its myriad social economic functions and their role in the trading activities during the medieval times. Both the Lohars and the Banjaras employ ox for travelling and transporting respectively. The major distinction amongst both is regarding the possession of cattle. The Banjaras own large number of bullocks whereas the Lohars will only rear the animal for fulfilling the dairy and load carrying activity. The Lohars employ the bullock in carts called *gaddas* (see Plates 1 and 2) and through usage of these *gaddas* the community acquired the popularity and became famous as *Gadiya/Gadariya Lohars*. The Lohars employ the ox in the carts which are huge, made in the chariot style and studded liberally with decorative pieces of copper carved in floral designs. It is a very common decorative design in Rajasthanai style furniture. On the other hand the Banjaras directly load bales on the bullocks by a double-loading technique.

A cursory look at the court manuscripts and the state and local revenue records helps us to understand a lot about the increasing demand for the expansion of the trade and trade activities. The state was extending support, assisting the merchants and was working constantly to enhance facilities en-route. Such as water arrangements and lodging facilities in the form of sponsoring the well digging on routes and construction of *sarais*. These kinds of incentives extended by the state for the merchants were impressive and ensured the safety on routes and definitely these facilities and safety measures were working more than an incentive to undertake the trade activities and expand the quantum of trade. Indirectly, it accelerated the process of community formations who were dedicated to the cause of trade and business. The *shroff/sarraf/sharoffs*, *hundi* and mints were integral to the trade activities and facilitated the movement of traders without risk of being looted. The safety mechanisms not only secured the investments of the traders but were also serving as motivating factors for undertaking and expanding the reach of trade activities.

The commercial vitality of medieval India appears more remarkable in view of the difficulties, which confronted the transportation of things during the period. In large parts of the country, especially in north-western India, traffic was somewhat thwarted and handicapped by the bad state of the roads. In the rainy season it must have been almost impossible to ferry things from one place to the other along roads that were quagmires of water and mud. The public authorities improved the infrastructure on the routes but did not seem to have made any attempt to improve the condition of the roads. Any progress accomplished in this matter appears to have been due solely to the initiative of travellers, pilgrims and merchants. Despite such daunting difficulties we come across merchants, either settled or passing through, at every halt or crossroads. As discussed above the fact was that the internal trade of India during the seventeenth and eighteenth centuries was quite vibrant. The glamour of maritime commerce[4] should not lead us to forget the importance of local and regional trade, about which much less is known. Since there is a shortage of sources, it has attracted less research. Small scale daily transactions either for cash or by barter necessarily left few traces in the archives. Generally speaking administrative records providing statistical data on local trade are not abundant. Only some records provide a sample of informative documents.

With the development of a vast agrarian society during the seventeenth century, internal trade circuits and networks were also formed. These inter-regional exchanges gave birth to an urban economy and commerce, which assumed a number of varied forms. Modifications were made in the community workings. Corresponding to these varied forms, there could be levels of organizations and a hierarchy of mercantile communities. Thus, there were settled merchants and nomadic groups operating medieval India's internal trade. The internal trade was better organized and more important and also served as feeder for the exports at the coastal towns and ports. The wealthy merchants linked together and formed the guilds and merged with the local merchant groups who were already dealing with the agrarian communities. The sole motive that guided these connections was to enhance profit and minimize the risk. Many nomadic groups were scattered all over the Indian subcontinent (Nahmardis, Rebaris, Kachis, Gosiyans, etc.). Ecologically dry, the north-west areas were suitable for development of a historically hardy, socio-economic organization or group and communities like the Banjaras, Raikas (shepherds) and Rebaris (camel keepers), etc. They formed a heterogeneous group given to rudimentary style of living and depended on livestock for their survival. The Banjaras became the most prominent nomadic group because they organized the transport of foodstuff by land on pack-oxen. Their endurance in travel and efficiency in transporting goods insured the Banjaras as the only 'supplying group' and 'transporting community'. Further, the community expanded its reach in forest and hill areas besides the dry and semi-arid lands from where they started. The feeling of love, dependence and war allowed them to associate and co-relate strongly with the various social groups who were a settled population and were specifically featured as controlled and regulated, living with the idea of 'state protection'. The exercise of 'Right to State Protection' often twisted the equation of protection against the local inhabitants because the Banjaras exercised their traditional right to graze the animal while travelling en-route, which often lead to quarrel and intervention of state was requested. It is clear that the economic motive of state pushed it to guide the favours and usually it was extended to the Banjaras. The favours were clubbed with the instructions for maintaining the mutual and symbiotic relationship. This was a method adopted by the state to suggest co-existence rather than annihilation. It was due to the economic significance of both the contenders. The state can't afford to lose any of the both. The favours to the Banjaras were mainly due to the nature of service provided by them to the state as the 'suppliers'. They also supplied the imperial armies during campaigns. The text narrates many interesting incidents where the Banjaras were supplying to the fighting armies in battlefields and at times accompanying them for maintaining the unbreakable supply chain. In this work an effort is being made to look at various aspects of the life of the Banjaras and highlight their significance in medieval Indian history; which has been denied for long.

The importance of the Banjara as a transporter can be judged from a line of Nazir Akbarabadi's poem 'Banjaranama'. It reads: '*Sab thaat para rah jawega, jab lad chalega Banjara*', i.e. 'all this paraphernalia will be left behind, when the Banjara packs up and departs'.[5] The poem is pointing to the spiritual sense of life and death. But it is of immense help to draw out the list of items traded and transported by

Banjaras. Interestingly, all the items mentioned in the poem are dry products. The massive commercial network of the medieval Indian history doesn't seem to work if the produce was not transported out of the area of production. The vast diverse geographical spread of India was providing conducive conditions to the cultivators for producing multiple crops, species, grains, pulses, vegetables and fruits. Many items were specific to the areas of cultivation. Certain areas produced surplus agrarian products and many zones were deficit in agricultural production. For example Gujarat was not producing any food grains (except for the odd bajara and jawar on its eastern boundary) and was completely dependent on Bengal and Awadh for food supplies. Similarly, Bengal and the eastern areas depended on Gujarat and Rajasthan for salt. The spices from peninsular India were supplied across the length and breadth of the continent. The saffron from Kashmir was a luxurious commodity for anyone in the continent. Supplies of dry fruits also had the same association. The merchants invested to procure produce from the cultivator. The diverse agricultural produce required an acquainted transportation system through which the products can be dumped in the markets and urban centres.

Herein, the Banjaras were inducted and they transported the items to the designated destinations. Overall, the Banjaras were the only connecting link who made the produce to reach the markets, through the investments of the traders, from where it was made accessible to the diverse consumers and waiting armies.

Somehow, the Banjaras have been assigned a peripheral role in the existing historiography. We only come across some passing remarks made by scholars in their otherwise scholarly works. C.A. Bayly has argued that the Banjaras were Hindu traders who transported mainly grains and salt on pack oxen.[6] Bayly, further notes that the zamindars normally sold their grain to the itinerant dealers and Banjaras who would take it to distant markets. Whenever the grain had to be delivered to meet the requirement of the fighting armies, garrisons, etc., security was provided by the royal forces. However, it appears that Banjaras themselves undertook the dual task of transport and safety whenever they were hired by merchants for long-distance supplies. He has suggested that the role of Banjaras was crucial in the economies of post-Mughal states but the Banjaras were subjected to a more limited role in the economy after 1800 in both

British and Indian territories. Thus the Banjaras who played an important role in the internal trade of the country for many centuries before India's colonization, were gradually eliminated from the commercial scene. The famous work of S.A.A. Rizvi, *The Wonder that was India*, has paid only cursory attention to the Banjaras by stating 'food grains were distributed by Banjaras or wandering grain dealers . . . on their bullocks . . . army and township depended upon the grain trader for their survival'.[7]

Irfan Habib finds the Banjaras as one of the mercantile communities who combined trading and pastoralist activities. They are put at par with the pastoral tribes of Sindh, Baluchistan and Himalayas. Habib rightly observes that the Banjaras were both Hindus and Muslims.[8] Tapan Raychaudhuri is of the view that the Banjaras organized the transport of foodstuffs by land on pack-oxen in large camps or *tandas* ranging between 12,000 and 20,000 bullocks capable of carrying 1,600 to 2,700 tons. The number of pack-oxen used by the Banjaras in a single journey indicates the high magnitude of this trade. Tapan Raychaudhuri also suggests an upward trend in the volume of Banjara trade.[9] However, in the absence of comparable quantitative data, it is not possible to verify the claims made by Raychaudhuri. Moreover, the scattered nature of the sources and the fact that these are not available in a continuous series has also impacted the certitude about some aspects of the life of the Banjaras. Nevertheless an attempt has been made in this work to bring in light certain aspects of the life of the Banjaras which have remained unattended hitherto. Sri Ram Sharma has tried to highlight the importance of the social organization of the Banjaras through their language and opines that the Banjaras are from Rajasthan and has marked their settlement area as a stretch ranging between Jaisalmer and Udaipur. His work is mainly based on the literature available in form of *Raso* and *Vats*. The literature used is mainly the collection of oral narratives collected by him during the field work in the areas around Hyderabad.[10]

This book is divided into five chapters. In the first chapter, the social organizations of the Banjaras have been discussed extensively. The festivals, rituals and other social practices form an integral part of any community and provide an insight into the beliefs and sect adherence of the community. As mentioned in the preceding section the Banjaras are a heterogeneous group and their religious affiliations guide their festivals, rituals and ceremonies. The Banjaras worship large number of gods, goddesses and local deities. Many ceremonies are performed which have been acquired from the varied cultural interactions. Undoubtfully, these celebrations provide a tool of understanding, for making notion of a community and these ceremonies bind the community into a strong and unbreakable togetherness firmly. The ceremonies performed at marriage, child-birth and death are extensive and very specific in conveying the messages of happiness and sadness respectively. In the second chapter, the role of Banjaras as transporter of foodstuff and other items has been discussed. The places where from they collected commodities and the centres of their destination have been identified. Maps have been provided for the assistance of readers. They indicate the various places and the routes which were accessed by the Banjaras. The safety and security of the commodities carried by the bullocks of a *tanda* were 'collective responsibility' of all the members in the *tanda*. The women were also entrusted with responsibility of security. The items carried by the *tanda* were mainly dry and non-perishable goods. The goods were mainly consignments of the merchants, traders and the state. Besides the transportation, the

Banjaras also undertook some trade and exchange activities inorder to subsidize the en-route *tanda* expenses and miscellaneous expenditures. The third chapter is devoted to description of the commodity structure of the Banjara trade. Here an attempt has been made to provide an idea about the volume of trade carried by Banjaras. In the fourth chapter en-route tensions between the Banjaras and the peasants, between the state and the Banjaras have been described. Some underlying causes of these conflicts have been identified. The reports and the *Arzdashts* indicate to a love and hate relationship, wherein both the peasants and the Banjaras were trying to contest and negotiate their rights and traditional rights respectively and the state was intervening constantly to moderate inorder to protect its own economic right. The instances indicating to the trio are interesting and have been attached in Appendix for providing detailed information to the reader and get a sense of the nature of struggles. The dispensing of justice was a tough task. So, the state meandered from harsh penalties to favours and did constant manoeuvring to maintain harmonious and symbiotic relationship between peasants on one hand and the Banjaras on the other. An effort has been made in the fifth chapter to understand the making of a criminal Banjaras as per the idea and labeling done by the East India Company, who in the initial years of their establishment in India employed Banjaras due to their effective mechanisms of transport and supply. Later in 1850, the same efficiency helped the Company to label Banjaras as a criminal tribe on account of the 'inability of surveillance' on the part of Company. I have concluded by making some observations about the character and significance of Banjara trade in the internal commercial world of medieval north-west India.

As stated earlier, the history of internal trade especially carried out by the tribes and nomadic groups, in medieval India is not well served by documentary evidences. Even there is little evidence to throw some light on the organization of the internal trade. On the other hand, we have next to no evidence to reveal its changing contours. Thus, the meagre evidences we have at our disposal cannot offer definitive answers to many questions. However, the relative dearth of the evidence should not lead us to underestimate the economic and social significance of the Banjaras, their trade and cultural practices.

This work is based on a variety of sources. Foremost

among them are the regional archival documents preserved in the Rajasthan State Archives at Bikaner. As groups of Banjaras frequently passed through Rajasthan, their activities were constantly recorded and reported by local state officials. Documents such as *Arzdashts, Chithiyat* and *Arsatthas*[11] contain useful information about the Banjaras. After an extensive and close perusal of these records, I was able to cull some relevant information focusing on the activities of the Banjaras. A large number of European travellers visited India from the sixteenth to the eighteenth centuries. Some of them managed to penetrate remote villages in the countryside. Observations made by European travellers in their accounts are of immense help in identifying the nature of Banjara trade and their lives. The memoirs of the British officials touring different parts of India, also contain useful information in this regard. The observations made by the factors of the English East India Company are helpful in knowing about the Banjaras and composition of *tandas*. Brief, but interesting commentaries made in some Persian chronicles have also enabled us to throw some light on some aspects of the life of the Banjaras. Additionally, relevant evidence from modern census reports has also been used to indicate the changing contours in the fortune of the Banjaras. *Mardumshumari* is a census report popular as the Marwar Census Report of 1891. It is a detailed collection of the castes living in the region of Marwar and also provides details about their respective histories and rituals. This text describes the Banjaras as *Baldiyas* (the ones who use the *balad*). *Balad* is a Marwari word for ox and *Aakil* stands for bull. The description of the Banjaras starts with the identification of community as a *kom* (community) who bring in and take away the goods especially salt. The leader of the community is called *Nayak* but in Marwar the *Naik/Nayak* is known as *Bigadu* (a spoiler) because the moving *carvans* and its animals (oxen) tend to spoil the fields and standing crops due to direct grazing. They constantly travel and always keep a stick in the hand. The stick is called *katal* derived from the word *qatal* (murder) and Banjaras are well equipped in using it for protection and safeguarding the *tanda*.[12] Interestingly, all the sources indicate towards certain common features like a constantly travelling group, a troop is referred as *tanda*, transporting dry items, the leader is known as *Nayak*, the use of ox, usage of double-loading technique, women and children accompanying on the travel.

With the development of agrarian society based on the surplus extraction by the state,[13] exchange networks emerged[14] and various forms of mercantile communities developed at different levels. Notable among these communities during the medieval centuries were the Baniyas and Banjaras. Baniyas were mainly associated with credit giving and taking, whereas the Banjaras undertook long-distance trading and transportation. The Banjaras took up the dual activities, i.e. pastoralism and carrying of trade. The role of Banjaras in Indian agrarian commerce was far more important and regular than that of the hill tribes (Bhotiyas in Himalayas, the Nahmardi traders of Sind and Baluchistan) living on the margins of the sub-continent.[15]

Banjaras were first described, with some essential details, by Barani in his account of the market reforms and price-control measures of Sultan Alauddin Khilji (*r.* AD 1296-1316). The sultan ensured that the peasants should sell the food grains to the *karavanis* (people of the *carvan*) at low and fixed prices who would transport the same to the Sultanate's capital. This arrangement was part of his larger fiscal reforms and military maintenance. The headmen of the *karavanis* were put in chains until they agreed to collect the food grains from the countryside and transport it subsequently to the sultan's granaries. The women, children and cattle of the *karavanis* were kept as hostage on the banks of Yamuna for ensuring their good conduct.[16] To ensure the collection of grains and faithful good conduct of Banjaras, their family and cattle were kept as hostage and state promised good care of them till the Banjaras return with the goods and grains collected from the countryside.

The commercial landscape of medieval India was marked by diverse mercantile communities transacting in a variety of commodities at variable prices on local, inter-regional and inter-provincial levels. The trading networks embraced both the agricultural and non-agricultural goods, based on a variety of markets organized in a hierarchy. There existed a variety of markets welding together the rural, semi-urban and urban localities. The extensive trading activities of medieval India are visible in various scholarly works, which are significant to draw the canvas of trade activities and the quantum of trade.[17] In this scheme, *mandis* which specialized exclusively in the wholesale trade occupied the largest space as the *mandis* were centres of collection, transaction, storage, exchange and delivery. In all this system the *mandis* gained prominence because these were the safe arenas guarded and protected by state but mainly controlled by the local traders in terms of business activities. Markets dealing in the grain and other merchandise with a cluster of shops (*hattis*) were situated in all the *qasbas* or towns. These were followed by bazaars comprising of numerous *hattis* dealing in retail and wholesale transactions. Further, lay the *katlas* which were also the wholesale markets of a permanent nature. Moreover, the weekly markets (*hatwaras* or *hats*) were also organized on fixed days. These varieties of markets were further supplemented by fairs (*melas*) held in particular periods of the year. During the medieval centuries, trade was flourishing and the profits from trade gave incentive to various castes to switch over to trade practices. The vigour, volume and velocity of trade depended entirely on the well organized and managed transportation system. The trading communities operating through these networks were the pivot of India's internal trade. It is needless to say that they managed this trade through multiple transport and carriage systems. While looking at the pre-colonial merchant communities, it seems that the two communities who dominated the Indian inland trade were Baniyas/Banias and

Banjaras. The Banias represented the group which invested money in trade. They extended credit to the various trading communities on interest. The Banias were largely associated with the prevalent buying, selling and credit systems. Specially, in the areas around markets and the trading towns, a lot of Banias settled and extended their credit activities. Some remarkable examples are visible in the towns of Nawalgarh and Ramgarh. Both townships have huge *bahi* records and closely knitted markets providing nearly everything from needle to sword. The town of Ramgarh is popularly known as Setho-ka-Ramgarh. The majority of traders here mainly belong to the famous Oswal merchant community who settled in the Churu district around fifteenth century and established this town in sixteenth century. The traders of both the towns (Nawalgarh and Ramgarh) travelled to distinctly placed trade and commercial centres and returned back home with the memories of different trading towns. The exposure to the distantly placed markets and urban centres like Kolkata and Mumbai were full of surprises and were more than enough to astonish the traders of the aforesaid small towns. On returning to their native townships the merchants and traders expressed their surprises and got them narrated through the painting designs popularly called '*Bhiti-Chitrikas*'; painted on the inner and outer walls of their *havelis* (the residential dwellings). The painting on the outer walls are open galleries for the locals to get a reflection of the other-outer progressive world where the merchants of their town had visited and has seen all the inventions like railways, uniformed standing armies, electric street lights, one horned Rhino, etc.

Contrary to the traders, the Banjaras represented a primitive collection of originally divergent group of people who undertook the transportation for largest portion of India's inland trade. The Banjaras played a crucial role as transporters during the medieval centuries. They had an immense control over the transportation of large quantities of goods in inland trade. In north-western India due to lack of waterways Banjaras played an active and significant role. But they were equally active in other regions of the country. The large number of oxen employed by them made it possible to transport large quantities of grains from place to place. Some scholars have exaggerated the number of cattle owned by Banjaras to be upto 1 lakh!

Badauni writing in the sixteenth century was the

first historian who mentioned about these transporters by the appellation of Banjara. He referred to them as grain-sellers, and called them 'the Banjaras of the Army'. He highlighted the social significance of the Banjaras by citing many instances of their non-arrival and the consequent hardships caused to the waiting army and other people.[18] Ferishta also confirmed this assessment by noting the role of Banjaras as suppliers to Sikander Lodi's expeditionary force in AD 1504.[19] Both these authorities made it clear that the Banjaras were active during the sixteenth century. Moreover, Badauni's observation helps us to know that the generic term Banjara had begun to be used by the beginning of the sixteenth century. Abul Fazal notes that the convoyers of grain, in the language of India are called Banjara.[20] Jahangir was also requesting the Banjaras to maintain an unbreakable chain of supplies to the moving army which was charging towards Qandahar for expedition.[21] During the early medieval period Banjaras were known as *Manpursha* (people of respect), as depicted in some inscriptions around Udaipur (Rajasthan). During the fourteenth and fifteenth centuries they were referred by the generic term *carvanis/karvanis*. I suppose this was because of their linear organization and movement of troops in a sequence. Probably the term Banjara was coined in sixteenth century due to the influence of Persian language. But, the noting of Abul Fazal indicates to Indian origin of the word. The word '*Brinj*' in Persian means rice and the carrier of rice is '*Brinjar*'. Another suggestion comes from the word '*ban*' which means forest and the Banjara is a forest wanderer. The later suggestion goes contrary to the origin of the community who has strong origin connect with the dry areas of the north-western region and the same is strongly enforced and depicted through usage of language and costumes. Many scholars have suggested varied derivations for the term but yet no clear origin and derivation identity has been established for the word 'Banjara'. The popular sub-group of the community is that of the Labanas, the section which trades in *lun* (salt). All the derivations are very vague and don't help to reach a conclusion. So, even now it is difficult to mark the single point of origin for the term Banjara. The Persian derivation is the nearest in terms of speech. The shift from the status of salt transporter to the transporter of large number of goods and outreaching travel through the forest routes breaking away from the limitation of dry areas; to make the supplies is a possible indicator for dropping the identity of Labana and taking up the wide identity of a Banjara.

An understanding of the extent and organization of the market for agricultural produce is necessary for any serious study of the nature of involvement of the Banjaras in it. A striking feature of the agrarian trade in Mughal India was a near non-dependence of the village on the produce of the town. Conversely, the towns absorbed a large portion of the produce of the villages. This was made possible due to the heavy land revenue demand. Land revenue under the Mughals was both in cash (*zabt* system) and in kind (*batai* system). The peasants sold part of their produce to pay revenue in cash. The state also had to sell its grain collected as revenue in kind under the *batai* system. This system generated a vast rural market in food grains. The involvement of state in grain trade and the market was significant as it controlled a sizeable grain stock. The need of state in terms of the grain was always very high. The large imperial armies needed the constant supply of *rasad* (food supply), arms and ammunitions, etc. The Banjaras also supplied other necessities to the army along with the grains. So, with assertion it can be said that the

Banjaras of medieval India also acted as auxiliaries of the army being the active transporters of goods.

The structure of these markets and the type of agencies which influenced their day to day working has been analysed by Madhavi Bajekal.[22] She has argued that the state and administration had substantial stakes in the marketing of food grains. The collection of revenue in kind was much in vogue. The state usually maintained huge granaries, locally known as *khasas* to store its collected revenue. This stored grain was sold to the traders on priority basis and on prices favourable to the state. In this process state was able to use the private traders as instruments for its own trading operations. The collection of the grains and agricultural produce on the ground of the production was a task assigned to the peasants and merchants worked as mediators and brokers and made the payments as fixed by the state. The parting of peasant from the produce was after making of the payment. The next step in the procurement was the collection of the produce from the fields or the *mandis*. The herculean task of picking up the grains from the collection point and to transport it to markets and urban centres was designated to the

Banjaras. This requirement made the Banjaras to halt around the areas of production and carry the consignment as per the instructions of the merchants, owners or the state. The visibility of Banjaras in the areas of Rajasthan, Uttar Pradesh, Maharashtra, Gujarat and Andhra Pradesh was very wide but they did not attach to any specific area and never settled in one place due to their job profile wherein they were required to be on the constant move. The various settlements of the native population described varied narratives and stories about the regular visits of Banjaras and specific zones that were allotted for halting of Banjaras and their bullocks. These halting zones were always kept away from the fields and were at a safe distance from villages too.

All records of sale contracts negotiated between the pargana administration and the traders were maintained by the local revenue officials.[23] These were organized chronologically, recording the details of sale held each day, village name, grain sold, purchaser's identity, quantity of crop sold and its sale price. The evidence suggests that the state's intervention in price setting was closely related to its role as the major seller of grain in the market. These sale deeds are recorded in the *Nirakh Bazaar* documents available in large number in the Jaipur Historical Section of the Rajasthan State Archives at Bikaner.

The fixing of bazaar prices by the state was more a process of bargaining between the local merchants and the political authorities. Further, the state intervention in negotiating retail price with wholesale price was a mechanism to ensure the smooth flow of grain into the towns. The supply was made through various transportation facilities available. Such as carts, direct loading on the animals like donkey, camel and mule, etc., but these mechanisms were successful only for the short distance transportation. Contrary to it, the Banjaras loaded directly on the ox and were proficient in travelling the far off distances, cutting through all the hurdles and risks offered by deserts, hills, forests and rivers. The use of animal power for grain transportation was most common in the region of our study. The Banjaras specialized in both, i.e. harnessing the animal power and transporting goods by ox over long-distances. This twin specialization made the Banjaras indispensable in the medieval economy.

The process of inter and intra-local trade made few markets famous for certain goods. A large number of commodities were supplied from the villages to small towns and big cities. These commodities included salt, spices, metal-ware, raw material of textiles, grains, ghee, etc. A striking feature of commerce is that all the urban centres had a large grain intake from the nearby villages. During this period certain regions produced some specific goods which were transported to the areas that did not produce these items. Similarly, grain production in some areas was less and was plentiful in other zones. Thus, an inter-regional trade between the surplus and deficit regions became necessary. For example Bengal was a surplus region for grain production. It supplied grain to various parts of the country. On the other hand Gujarat which specialized in the production of textiles and handicrafts exchanged these items for grain from other parts of India. Before the advent of Banjaras the natives depended mainly upon the local produce. The vibrancy of the consumption was achieved due to the efforts of the Mughals who protected and supported the trade activities, as the flourishing trade benefited the state treasury in form of the taxes and revenue collections. It may, however, be stated here that all trading goods did not pass through the hands of the Banjaras. A large part of inter-regional trade depended on the riverine and coastal routes because of the enhanced speed and low cost. The waterways, both riverine and littoral were comparatively cheaper and therefore preferred.[24] However, transport through the water ways could not be perennial. We find that much of the riverine trade was during the month of *Sawan* (rainy season), when the level of water in the river usually made an upward movement. Obviously, the drying of river puts its own limitations on the quantity of the riverine trade. Hence, the role of the Banjaras was largely confined to dry lands and distant difficult terrains. The diverse geographical settings made specific kinds of transporters popular in different regions. In western India the waterways are scarce and seasonal; therefore, these were not at all popular as a mode of transportation. Here the bulk of intra-regional and inter-regional trade and transportation relied on the pastoral groups, such as Banjaras and Rebaris. The former employed oxen and the latter used camel for their respective trading and transporting operations.

The Banjaras were preferred over the camel traders because of the low cost of transportation done by pack-oxen, through the technique of 'Double-loading'.[25] Secondly, the loading and unloading of camel was comparatively a difficult task. Bullock carts were also used overland as a means of transport for goods. But due to the various restrains that didn't allowed to accelerate the speed of carts, the pack-oxen were most preferred means of transportation. The bullocks with loads neither require a smooth path nor an even road, which was an essential requirement for the movement of a loaded cart, to ensure the safety of the goods which can turn upside down while crossing over the pitted and treacherous muddy roads. The hoof of the ox is small and due to its strong grip the cattle is able to climb up the hills and walk down the slopes easily by balancing the weight effectively. The animal is also a small grazer and survives effectively on the various varieties of the route side grasses. No special grazing and resting place was required. A small amount of water at the end of the day would be sufficient to keep the cattle going. Camels were also used for carrying goods especially between Agra and Surat. However, the camels were considered inferior to bullock carts and bullocks, as they took longer time and it was a troublesome task to directly load a camel. Secondly, the cart used for the camel was huge and heavy and needed maintenance of a peculiar kind to withstand the hunching movements of the camel. The camel-cart can't afford even a minor error.

The maps and images in this book both intend to contemplate and supplement the text. The names, spellings of the places are as per modern usage. The boundaries of the *subas* and *sarkars* are not provided as the purpose of map was to provide the routes used by the Banjaras. The information for the same is collected from various sources. The making of the routes over the rivers are indicative of the fact that these rivers were crossed with boat bridges and many a times the receding water in non-monsoonal months proved helpful.

Thus, to conclude, it can be mentioned that comparative cost benefit, speed and efficiency left the Banjaras as the big transporters who controlled the major part of internal trade. The magnitude of trade carried by them suggests a near monopoly in the inland trade. Normally, the Mughal state officials maintained regular contacts with the Banjaras for organizing some specific supplies of goods from place to place. Many Banjaras accompanied the royal troops. There were some special people and organizations recognized by the Jaipur state who maintained regular contacts with the Banjaras which helped them to regularize internal and external trade.

Colonialism has destroyed many specialized

communities and divested them from their historic, political, social, economic and cultural attributes in the twentieth century. The Banjaras also met the same fate as the Beldars of Purniya and Nuneas of Saran who lost their professions and livelihoods due to John Company.[26] The Banjaras remained an 'open to manipulation conflict group', which was later fit into the Criminal Tribes and Eunuchs Act of 1871. The community didn't not push its judicial claim due to its traditional reliance on the community panchayat for settling all the personal and public matters. The same situation prevails in the twenty-first century. The community is living a life of ignorance and is not visible on the political platforms due to scattered settlement (on government lands, which the authorities refer as 'unauthorized possession') of its population in diverse and distant corners of the country. The community is unable to come out in a united manner because of its insignificant economic status and lack of organization and leadership. The community awaits the wake-up of government so that they can plea for their identity as citizens and can at least get identity cards, ration cards and the adhaar numbers which are not allotted to the free wanderers because they have no legal place to settle and no bank accounts to merge in with the visionary mission of digital India. The absence and scarcity of evidence is a huge hurdle in accessing the contribution of the community to the Indian subcontinent and its much decried economy! But the hope lies in the re-evaluation of the old evidences and keeping a keen eye for search of minors (the neglected ones) and their contribution in the major historical themes. The Banjaras and their contribution is a neglected aspect of history writing. In the following chapters a modest attempt has been made to describe various aspects of the social and economic life of the Banjaras who were operating in the long distance trade, mainly in the north-western region of India during the sixteenth, seventeenth and eighteenth centuries.

NOTES

1. Burton Stein, *A History of India*, Oxford University Press, New Delhi, 7th impression, 2009, p. 6.
2. Ibid., p. 13.
3. Malavika Kasturi, *Embattled Identities: Rajput Lineages and the Colonial State in Nineteenth-Century North India*, Oxford University Press, New Delhi, 2002.
4. Ashin Das Gupta, *The World of Indian Ocean Merchants c. 1500-1800,* Oxford University Press, New Delhi, 2004.
5. 'Banjaranama' is an eleven stanza narrative poem written by the noted Urdu poet, Nazir Akbarabadi (AD 1735-1830). In

it, the Banjara is depicted as a worldly person whose success can be seen in the quantity and range of goods he carries for sale. It is important for understanding the public perception about the Banjaras. The poem appears in full in *Intikhab-i-Nazir Akbarabadi* (Maktaba Jamia, New Delhi, 1970), pp. 106-9. See Appendix I, Poem 'Banjara'.

6. C.A. Bayly, *Rulers, Townsmen and Bazaars: North Indian Society in the Age of British Expansion c. 1770-1870,* Cambridge University Press, New Delhi, 1983, p. 221. Here after *Rulers, Townsmen and Bazaars.*
7. S.A.A. Rizvi, *The Wonder That Was India: A Survey of the History and Culture of the Indian Sub-continent from the Coming of the Muslims to the British Conquest c. 1200-1700,* vol. II, Picador India, London, 2005, p. 207.
8. In 1891, in the N.W. Province (U.P.) there were 26,957 Muslims in a total of 66,828 Banjaras. For further details see, Irfan Habib, 'Merchant Communities of Pre-colonial India', in James D. Tracy (ed.), *The Rise of Merchant Empires 1350-1750,* Cambridge University Press, Cambridge, 1990, p. 10. Here after 'Merchant Communities'.
9. The popular means of transport during medieval times were boats on the rivers and ships on the coastal routes and bullock-carts, pack-oxen and camel on the inland routes. For details see Tapan Raychaudhuri, 'Inland Trade', in Tapan Raychaudhuri and Irfan Habib (eds.), *The Cambridge Economic History of India c. 1200-1750*, vol. I, Orient Longman, New Delhi, 1982, pp. 325-59.
10. Sri Ram Sharma, *Banjara Samaaj,* Dakshin Parkashan, Hyderabad.
11. The *Chithis* were written by the *Diwan* of Amber state to officials particularly to the *amils* and *faujdars*. These *Chithis*

contain complains received by the *Diwan* and his instructions thereon.

The *Arzdasht* was written by *amil* and *faujdar* and other officials of Amber state, posted in various parganas. The *Arzdashts* were addressed to the raja of Amber in form of supplications. These documents contain information regarding the prevailing social, political and economic conditions. *Arzdashts* are the documents of some importance on the everyday movement of the Banjaras.

Arsatthas are revenue records. For details see Appendix II.

12. Rai Bahadur Munshi Hardayal Singh, *Report Mardum-shumari: Marwar Census Report, 1891: History and Rituals of Castes of Rajasthan*, Maharaja Mansingh Pustak Parkashan, Mehrangarh, Jodhpur, rpt. 2010, pp. 443-5.
13. Irfan Habib, *The Agrarian System of Mughal India,* Oxford University Press, New Delhi, 1999, 2nd edn. Here after *ASMI.*
14. G.S.L. Devra, 'Sources on Trade and Trade-routes of Western Rajasthan (1780-1848)', in N.S. Bhati (ed.), *Sources of Socio-Economic History of Rajasthan and Malwa (1700 to 1900 AD),* Maharaja Man Singh Pustak Prakashan, Jodhpur, 1989, pp. 52-7.
15. Irfan Habib, 'Merchant Communities', in James D. Tracy (ed.), *The Rise of Merchant Empires c. 1350-1750*, Cambridge University Press, Cambridge, 1990, p. 4.
16. Zia-Barani, *Traikh-i-Firuz-Shahi*, ed. Saiyid Ahmad Khan, Bib. Ind., Calcutta, 1862, pp. 305-7, cf. Irfan Habib, 'Merchant Communities', op. cit., p. 5.
17. Habib and Raychaudhuri, *The Cambridge Economic History of India c. 1200-1750,* vol. I; Nandini Sinha Kapur, *State Formation in Rajasthan: Mewar during the Seventh-Fifteenth*

Centuries, Manohar, New Delhi, 2002; Jagat Narayan, *Ajmer and the Mughal Emperors*, Neha Vikas Prakashan, Kota, 1997.

18. Adbul-Qadir Badauni, *Muntakhab-ul-Tawarikh,* 3 vols., tr. George S.A. Ranking (1898 rpt., Delhi, Idarah-i-Adabiyat-i Delhi, 1973), vol. I, 477, vol. II, 240.
19. R.G. Varady, 'North Indian Banjaras: Their Evolution as Transporters', *South Asia Journal of South Asian Studies,* 1979, p. 3.
20. Abul Fazal, *Akbarnama*, tr. H. Beveridge, vol. 3, Low Price Publication, Delhi, 2011 (rpt.), p. 212.
21. *Tuzuk-i-Jahangiri*, tr. Alexander Rogers, and ed. Henry Beveridge, vol. 2, Low Price Publication, Delhi, 2006 (rpt.), pp. 233-4.
22. Madhavi Bajekal, 'The State and the Rural Grain Market in Eighteenth Century Eastern Rajasthan', *The Indian Economic and Social History Review,* 1988, p. 451.
23. Ibid., these officials belonged to the Jaipur state.
24. Raychaudhuri, op. cit., p. 329.
25. Varady, op. cit., p. 3 and see Plate 12.
26. N.P. Singh, 'The Deplorable Condition of Saltpetre Manufacturers of Bihar, 1773-1833', in Sabyasachi Bhattacharya (ed.), *Essays in Modern Indian Economic History*, Munshiram Manoharlal, New Delhi, 1987, pp. 102-7.

CHAPTER ONE

Social Organization of the Banjaras

ACCORDING TO THEIR own tradition, the Banjaras trace their origin from Rupa, a Rajput jagirdar of Rail Mangra near district Udaipur in Rajasthan. At some stage they left the place and began to lead a nomadic life with their occupation of trading. The Banjaras are mostly carriers and drivers of pack-bullocks. Though the name Banjara was first used in the sixteenth century, its origin is still a matter of debate. The British officials' memoirs, travel accounts and the colonial official reports, vary over the origin root of the word Banjara. Denzil Ibbetson opines that the Banjara term is derived either from the word *'Banij'* which means a trader or from *'Banji'* which stands for 'a pedlar's pack'.[1] The origin root of both the words

'*Banij*' and '*Banji*' is from the Sanskrit word '*Vanij*' which relates to the commercial activity. Henry M. Elliot, strongly suggests their Sanskrit origin from the word '*Banij*' which means a merchant.[2] He does not agree with Shakespear's dictionary which speculates about the Persian connection of its origin, in which '*Biranjar*' is 'a rice-carrier'. Elliot, clearly states that the word Banjara has a greater antiquity and therefore could not have any connection with Persia.[3]

While discussing the linguistic derivation of the term Banjara, various combinations have been proposed by scholars. Some of these are as follow:

1. *Vana* + *Jara* = Jungle wanderer (vana = jungle/ forest)
2. *Vanik* / *Banik* = Merchant
3. *Vanijya* / *Banijya*-kara = Merchant
4. *Banij* = a trader, etc.

I assume that the different usages of 'V' and 'B' to mark the words are influenced by the different speeches of dialects and languages, i.e. Rajasthani and Bangla, wherein Vinita is Binita, Vinod is Binod respectively. Similarly while travelling in between the land tract of Rajasthan and Bengal, the Banjaras might have picked some popular words and the pronunciation went on changing as per the crossings of boundaries. H.A. Rose opines that 'Wanjara is doubtless only another form of the name'.[4]

The last origin root is most acceptable to the scholars. Etymologically the word Banjara seems to be derived from *banijya* + *kar*, which means 'a merchant', also from '*ban-jarna*' which means 'burner' or 'cleaner of forest' or 'forest-wanderer', in which the last is not tenable. Though, the word 'Banjara' was used for the first time during the sixteenth century, these long distance carriers were first described with some essential detail during the reign of Sultan Alauddin Khilji for effective implementation of the price-control measures and market reforms, which became possible only after bringing in the grains and agricultural produce to the city, that too in designated time. The efficacy maintained in supply and effective delivery helped the Banjaras to maintain the regular supply to the city. Due to it the demand and supply remained stable and monetary and fisical regularization became possible. And, subsequently the economy was pushed towards relative stability. Here Barani has described them as *karavanis* (literally people of the *carvan*).[5] William Irvine collects them as Banjara (trader) or Birinjara (rice carrier).[6]

The Banjaras are also called by various other names like *Manaris,*[7] *Mukeri, Labana,*[8] *Wanjari* and *Baldia.*[9] The *Baldia* is called after the Hindi word *Bel* used for oxen; and *Baldia* means 'one who employs an ox'. In Karantaka the word *Baldia* becomes *Banijigaru* which means *Banjara.*[10] Some of these names are clear reflection of the articles and goods which were transported by Banjaras, like Labana is very close to *Lun*; which means salt in Marwari.

Some information about the social life of Banjaras is available in sixteenth-eighteenth centuries European travellers' accounts and British official reports. The British ethnographers postulated neat hierarchies among the Banjaras, basing it on the origin tales recited by tribal bards. They accepted these recitations on their face value. Each new permutation was treated as a separate Banjara class. This had split the Banjaras in numerous *gotras*. Thus, in the eyes of the ethnographers, various castes and classes are covered by the broader Banjara appellation. Elliot says that the original horde of Banjaras living in the northern forests has become much intermixed with other classes and men of all tribes were constantly deserting their homes and joining the Banjara fraternity.[11] Interesting instance is noted by H.A. Rose 'they have a tradition that Akbar dismissed Chaudhri Shah Quli from his service where upon he turned trader or Banjara'.[12] These tribal fugitives joined the Banjara fraternity as it provided respect and profits from trade. Broadly speaking, Elliot divides the Banjaras into six groups, namely, Turkia, Bayd, Labanas, Mukeri, Bahrup and Rathors.[13] Along with these broad groups, the *gotra* and the native place of a particular group are also noted.[14] Tavernier gives four major division of the Banjara community basing his classification on the goods transported by each group.[15] The four divisions are: (i) Supplier of corn (ii) Transporters of rice (iii) Pulse traders and (iv) Salt traders. Though it is an interesting way of grouping them, in reality, such neat barriers based on the traded commodity did not exist among the Banjaras. Might be the *carvans* were classified internally on basis of the produce or product carried by each animal. It must have been a feature to organize the trade in a better style and to prevent the inter-mixing of the items carried by the ox. This is due to the fact that each *tanda* traded in many commodities and variety of items and each consignment had a different delivery point. The *tanda* was organized by keeping in mind the items and their dump points. No *carvan* had exclusive trading rights of a particular commodity. This classification might have been done so that the goods can be unloaded as per the details of consignment and demands of each market, without much trouble of sorting the goods from back of each ox at the time of unloading. Further, the whole *carvan* need not to be unloaded and loaded; and only the required items on the back of bullocks will be taken into the *mandis*, leaving rest of the *carvan* bulls and members at the halting place. Indirectly, these planning and arrangements helped in saving time and at the same time helped the *carvans* to manage their day to day affairs of cooking, washing, resting, etc., effectively.

The Marwar census report of 1891 gives a clear picture of the castes which are covered by the Banjara appellation particularly those who belonged to Rajasthan.

They are broadly divided into eight groups along with their sub-groups:[16]

1. Bhats: Bagora, Bamaniya and Maru
2. Charans: Kachaila and Maru.

3. Rajputs: Rathors, Bhati, Guoda, Dahima, Padihar, Devada, Chawhan, Solanki, Jawada, Gaylada, Mun, Chadiya, Sodha and Dhukad.
4. Muslim: Multani
5. Gawariya
6. Gugad Gawar
7. Jat
8. Labana: Bishnois who shaved their heads.

In the areas around Amritsar the Banjara community is identified with *gauts* namely Manhas, Khokhar and Bhatti.[17] All these *gauts* are popular Rajasthani Rajput clans and it could be that these Banjara groups are descendants from the respective Rajput clans.

Explaining the internal structure of Banjaras a British official Mr. Cumberlege gives four main divisions of their caste in Berar (central India). These are: the Charans, Mathurias, Labhanas and Dharis.[18] The Charans are the bards who recite the family history of their patron. The Charans are further divided into Rajput clans of Rathors, Panwars, Chauhans, Puris and Jadons. They occupied the most important place among the Banjaras. The adoption of Rajput clan names suggests the inter-mixing of castes. Apparently, Charans who were affiliated to various Rajput clans adopted the name of their patron's clan. The commonly appearing names are Labanas, Multanis, Chauhans and Rathors. Various examples appear where the Banjara have suffixed the name of place to their groups to specify their native lands.

For example the Mathuria Banjaras are from Mathura. They are distinct from the Charan Banjaras both in their food habits and clothing. The Labanas and the Dharis explain their mythological connections with some unnamed solar dynasties as a common source of their origin.[19] However, R.V. Russell's explanation about the origin of the Banjara community from the Charans and Bhats does not appear to be true. Both the Charans and Bhats lived a sedentrized life and earned more money as courtiers.[20] Why should such a prosperous community shift to a nomadic life full of hazards and uncertainty?

The social history of varied groups and castes of Banjaras becomes more complex when we come to the discussion of their religion. Historians are divided in their opinion whether they were Hindus or Muslims. C.A. Bayly considers Banjaras solely to be Hindu merchants.[21] However, a close scrutiny of the travellers' accounts, British official memoirs and regional archival sources unmistakably indicate that Muslims also formed a part of this community. It may be stated here that the sources of the Mughal Empire contain little information about the religion and customs of the Banjaras. Interestingly, some Banjaras had also become Nanak Panthi. During the siege of Sadhaura, the Sikhs, when faced with acute shortage of provisions obtained what they could from the grain dealers with the royal army. The grain dealers attached to the imperial army were normally Banjaras.[22] Some of them had become Nanak Panthis. As a matter of interest it may be mentioned here that among the three Hindu Banjara tribes of the Deccan, a legend existed. In these stories Guru Nanak, the founder of Sikh religion usually figures as the opportune miracle worker, who blessed these tribes in their ventures and by performing miracles helped them to attain success. Though the *Charans* were known to be deists, they looked upon Guru Nanak as the supreme one. The Banjaras of central India say that their religion is that of the Sikhs.[23] Russell emphasizes the observation made by Balfour 'that Banjaras call themselves Sikh'.[24] Further, Cumberlege stated 'that before starting his marriage the bridegroom ties a rupee in his turban in honour of Guru Nanak, which is afterwards expended in sweetmeats'.[25] Noting carefully while visiting *tandas* I couldn't find presence of any such ritual these days with Banjaras or this might be absent in the *tandas* of Rajasthan. Even, the *carvan* members resist to recall any such tradition.

Tavernier's testimony that they were Hindu idolaters appears to be the sole source for Bayly. The Banjaras described by Tavernier had a priest and a serpent like idol carried on a staff on a special ox (called *goda* in Rajasthan). The duty of the priest was to place and remove the idol from the back of the bullock. Denzil Ibbetson notes about the Banjaras of the North-Western Provinces who were coming annually to Jammu and eastern states (with the letters of credit) to buy large number of cattle for the approaching summer season and they all were Hindus. According to Ibbetson all the Muslim Banjaras were peddlers.[26] While noting about the fourth sub-division, i.e. Dharis, Russell tells us how after attending a feast given by Mughal Emperor Humayun, the ancestors (Bhats) of Dharis became Muslim. They ate beef and got circumcised. According to a popular legend these Muslims worship Saraswati. However, a *fakir* is called to recite the prayers at the time of burial.[27]

According to Sir Henry Elliot, Turkia and Mukeri were two principal Muslim groups. The Turkia Banjara claim that they originally came from Multan and settled in their chosen country of the Deccan wherefrom under the leadership of Rustam Khan they re-joined the imperial armies.[28] Whereas, the Mukeri Banjaras of Bareilly assert that they derived their name from Mecca, which became corrupted into *Mukeri* due to their name's association with *Meccai* (maize).[29] The names of *Mukeri* Banjaras show us a combination of Hindu and Muslim tribes. Even the burial and crematory rituals explained in the Marwar census report suggests that the Banjara comprised of both the Hindus and Muslims.[30] A section of Banjaras buried their dead while the others cremated. The presence of 5-6 isolated *chhattris* in the Guriya village of Sikar district made me curious to find out about the importance of these *chhattris*. While, talking to people around the village I came to know that these are called *Banjara ki Chhattri* locally; which means they belonged to some Banjara group who had a popular Rajput link and on their death as a popular Rajput custom the *chhattris* were constructed to commemorate their memory.[31] In the *Arsattha* of pargana Lalsot for the year 1737, the name of the leader of a Banjara party has been recorded as Nayak Haider Mani. The presence of a number of Muslim Banjara names in our records clearly indicates that the community did not belong to any single religious denomination. Similarily, the names of the women members are also reflecting a mix of Hindu and Islamic names.[32]

Despite, their constant movement the Banjara community as a whole regularly observed its rituals, offered sacrifices and celebrated festivals. They also followed elaborate ceremonies and rituals related to child birth, marriages[33] and death.[34] The forms of worship followed by Muslim Banjaras are not recorded anywhere. Only the presence of a *fakir* or a learned man at the time of burial is usually mentioned in our sources. The *tandas* stationed around district Sikar, Udaipur, Jhunjhunu and Bikaner were interviewed while the research work was in progress. Some of these groups mentioned about the rituals associated and the precaution to be taken while applying henna (*mehndi*) which indicates to the Islamic influence. The collection of *chiragi* is another popular ceremony in the *carvans*, which is reflective of the Islamic traditions. Even the Hindu groups of Banjaras follow some of these rituals. Whereas, on the other hand the Hindu Banjaras are recorded to be worshippers of a large variety of gods, goddesses and deities. The various deities worshipped by the Banjaras are: serpent in the form of an idol,[35] Banjari Devi, Mithu Bhukia, Shiva Bhaia, Hatadiya.[36] Their kul devi is Gajana Mata.[37] The serpent idol is the image of a popular deity, i.e. Gogaji widely worshipped in Rajasthan. The worship of Gogaji is done for the well being of animals specially to keep animals safe from snake bites which is the most common danger in those parts. The Indian landscape has a large variety of venomous snakes. The worship of Gogaji is a simple ritual without elaborate ceremonies. The deity is worshipped by drawing a sketch on the wall where three serpents (see Plate 13) were drawn in *roli* (red colour), *kajal* (black colour) and *ghee* (saturated fat) respectively. The offering made to the deity is of milk. All these drawings and offering are indicators of the animals and their dairy products. The danger posed to animals by the venomous creatures made them worship Gogaji who would keep the cattle safe. Many other such deities are still worshipped by the farmers and people who mainly trade in animals and animal products. Some of these deities popular in Rajasthan are Sunder Das, Hiramal, Tejaji, Bhaguta Sidji.[38] The interesting fact is that all these deities are represented through the sketch of a serpent (a common representation) but the offerings (*prasad*) are with little variation and inevitably all made out of milk. The worship of Hatadiya deity in reality is a worship of the ox which obviously played a central role in the life of the Banjaras. A close study of our source material further helps us to know that the deities, gods and goddesses kept changing from place to place as the Banjaras travelled and moved ahead on their ways. However, the Banjara never failed to pray the deities of their native place. Our sources and the current practices observed in *tanda*; both clearly indicate that in medieval times the Banjaras largely worshipped those deities which had some association with animal power and were known for having the healing qualities. Ensuring safety on the routes and protection of oxen was the major motivation behind the worship of such deities.

But in modern times the Hindu Banjaras are inclining more towards the worship of deities connected with royal Rajput houses. These deities are: Jogmaya, Kalka, Gogaji, Ramdeviji[39] and Rani Bhatiyani.[40] It may, however, be mentioned here that all these deities had a folk origin. According to

Dominique-Sila Khan, the beginning of 'Rajputization' of these folk-deities can be traced back to the work of Mahto Nainsi, though the process acquired momentum only in the eighteenth century. Non-Rajput and popular elements can still be deciphered. Rajput values that were later brought to bear on the narratives can similarly be identified.[41]

Rani Bhatiyani who became a *sati* is the only deity with a royal ancestry. She was associated with the Bhatti rulers of Jaisalmer. The worship of Rani Bhatiyani, reveals the existence of Sati worship among the Banjaras. *Satis* were worshipped as they are reputed to possess healing and spiritual powers. Their names are invoked to get boons of male child and for keeping children safe from deadly diseases like, *choti mata* (small pox), *badi mata* (chicken pox). The worship of Mithu Bhukia who is alleged to be a Banjara Robinhood, is only the privilege of the male Banjaras who wished for a successful robbery.[42] The offerings to Mithu Bhukia are in the form of liquor and very specific male-goat meat. Ever since a section of the Banjaras took to robbery during the colonial period, the worship of Mithu Bhukia has become prevalent in modern times. Shiva Bhaia the other male deity which is a form of Lord Shiva is also popular among the Banjaras.[43] Thus, Shakti worship too appears to be widely prevalent among the Banjaras. Apart from the worship and ritualistic offerings to the multiple deities; the community also performed various evil practices like child sacrifice, women sacrifice, human sacrifice and witch craft.[44] The Banjaras firmly believe that these sacrifices would entail success in their trade. The most popular spiritual deities across all the Banjara groups are Pir Baba and Baba Ramdevji. Geographically, both the pilgrimage centres are located in district Nagaur of Rajasthan. Nagaur district is bordered by seven districts of Rajasthan namely Bikaner, Pali, Jodhpur, Jaipur, Churu, Ajmer, and Sikar. Interestingly, all these district are either important trading centres or centre of spiritual attraction and political power. Most importantly all these districts are major centre of trade exchange. The significance of these districts will be highlighted while discussing about the trade routes in a later chapter.

The Banjaras consider marriage as an important institution for the perpetuation of their family tree. The fixing of marriage amongst the Banjaras was based on the *gotra* system. The marriages are usually held in the month of *sawan* (rainy season) because it is a season devoid of trade and trading activities. The marriage ceremonies were performed with elaborate rituals.[45] The month of *sawan* in which the Banjaras organize engagements and marriages of young boys and girls is astrologically not considered to be a auspicious month for such purposes by other Hindus. The Banjaras think that their gods and goddesses become active during the month of *Sawan*. Though widow re-marriage is permitted amongst the Banjaras, such marriages are confined within the family; either to the younger or elder brother of the deceased male. The widows are normally not allowed to marry outside the family. In case the family agrees to marry her into an outside family, such marriages can happen only after paying a fee to the *nayak* (leader) of the *tanda*.[46]

Each Banjara *carvan* consisted of a large number of people. In course of their travel and staying together many disputes arose around issues such as marriage settlement, bull fights and fodder distribution. The settlement of all these disputes within the community was the responsibility of the Banjara *Panchayat*.[47] The *Panchayat* consisted of one *sarpanch* and a group of *panchas*, whose number kept varying. The selection of *panchas* for the settlement of any dispute was based on the choice of the disputing parties. The *sarpanch* was usually an elder Banjara who was chosen by the concerned *carvan*. The *panchas* were reputed and loyal Banjaras of the *carvan* who got selected on the basis of their ability to negotiate and mediate for settling the disputes, to make peace and restore harmony. The Banjaras normally avoided approaching the state institutions for the settlement of their disputes. Even today, Banjaras avoid going to the legal courts for settling their inter community disputes.

The process of adjudication of any case is a complex matter among the Banjaras. At the time of holding a *panchayat*, the *panchas* wear round earrings (*kundal*) and then petitioners put a stick in front of the *panchayat* for getting justice. The judgement of such *panchayats* was acceptable to all the concerned parties. If anybody disobeyed the judgement he was subjected to financial penalty and severe thrashing which was usually sufficient to force him to accept the judgement.[48] The entire process appears to be a hangover of an earlier tradition. During the medieval times the Banjaras had developed the notorious habit of kidnapping children whom they sold to earn money.[49] They also admitted these kidnapped children in their *tandas*, as concubines, slaves and servants.[50] For this reason the villagers always suspected that the Banjaras were practicing theft, kidnapping and witchcraft. Hence, their *tanda* was not allowed to encamp in the proximity of the village and exclusive halting zones away from villages were designated. Some of these areas are still famous and even now in continuity are known as *tanda*; the popular ones are the *tandas* at Gorakhpur, in Shimla, in Bikaner and Sikar. Looking at the Census Report of Government of India, I was able to locate 94 *tandas* around city of Aurangabad (Maharashtra), 11 around Rampur (Uttar Pradesh), 9 in surroundings of Bhopal, 8 around Kangra (Himachal Pradesh) and 27 in the surroundings of Faizabad (Uttar Pradesh). All these are medieval cities formed in seventeenth or eighteenth century.[51]

The Banjara community is reputed for their colourful dressing style and profusion of jewellery. Their dressing pattern is more influenced by the Rajput style. The dresses of women are quite fascinating which includes long skirts (*ghaghara*), blouse (*kachali*), dupatta (*odhani/lugadi*).[52] All the apparels are decorated with embroidery, glass pieces woven into them and various decorative designs made with cowries and beads. The cowries are a favourite ornament of Banjara women. The ornaments of women are made of silver in bell shaped designs. The ornamented head-dress (*chunda*/*chund*) worn by married Banjara women is the most fascinating part of their dress. The *chund* (elevated cone) thus provides a special identity exclusive to all married Banjara women. The *chund* is shaped like a horn. The angle of the horn indicates the status of women in the Banjara society.[53] For instance a woman who wore her *chund* in a straight form was usually of a higher status in the *tanda* and might be wealthier than others.

The two ornaments namely *chunda* (horn) and the *chuda* (the bangles made of ivory, worn above elbow and wrist) are particularly used by married women. The use of these ornaments is prohibited for unmarried girls. Barring these two, unmarried girls can wear any other ornament. Nowadays instead of the ivory bangles, the Banjara women are found wearing white plastic bangles. This usage of plastic and ivory bangles is also popular amongst the Kalbailiyas; another nomadic group in Rajasthan who are snake-charmers by profession and their women are proficient dancers. The famous Kalbailiya dancer Gulabo Kalbailiyan hailed from this group. The rising usage of plastic bangles is indicative of the increasing poverty amongst the Banjaras and deterioration in their status. On the other hand the ivory trade is no more legal; that is also one of the major reasons to abstain from usage of ivory. Even in this state of poverty, the Banjaras claim that they don't wear artificial jewellery and the claim is also refelected in their living tradition. The metals used for jewellery by them are gold and silver only.[54] The men wear *dhoti* and *kurta* with the silver *ta'awiz* (amulet).[55] The Banjara men who are rich and have high status in the *carvan* also wear gold earnings.[56]

A look at the social customs and organization of the Banjaras helps us to know that despite the community's constant movement, the Banjaras observed their customs and rituals regularly. My personal contact with the members of Banjara community and various long visits to the *tanda* gave me better insight into their social organization, rituals and festivals.

Though their lifestyle has changed considerably over time, the community still possesses fascinating traces of their past. Despite their sedentrization there is a visible continuity in the social customs of the Banjaras. In the absence of definite information regarding the social organization and customs of the Banjaras in the medieval sources, it is not possible to specify the contours of change overtime. Only the work of R.V. Russell written during the early twentieth century helps us to know a bit about the social life of the Banjaras. Even with such severe limitations of sources an effort has been made here to bring forward an authentic portrait of Banjara culture. I reiterate here that I extensively interviewed the members of a Banjara *carvan* in order to overcome the acute shortage of information in our sources regarding their social practices. Incidentally located in a marriage celebration, the following folklore popular among the Banjaras and other communities clearly highlights the important role of the Banjara women in the organization and working of their *tandas:*

Banjari yai tu soya mat ja; tando tharo lad jaasi,
Banjara ro balokdo subav; kiya tu tanda pache raisi,
Banjari yai tu soya mat ja; ki tando tharo lad jaasi,
Tanda la balad hazaar; tu to bane ghairan aali.

Banjari (wife of Banjara)! you don't fall asleep; Otherwise your *tanda* (troop) will be lost or loss way
The Banjara is bad tempered; so you stay at end of the *tanda*

Please Banjari! don't fall asleep; otherwise the *tanda* will be lost
There are thousand oxen into *tanda*; you shepherd them all.

Over all the social organizations suggests that the Banjaras were a nomadic community but were not devoid of the ceremonies, celebrations and rituals. Over the centuries their profession have changed but the continuity is visible in the customs.

The similar ceremonies and rituals of Hindu, Muslim and Sikh communities are indication to the fact that the Banjaras have adopted these rituals, from the respective group, to which they have either attached or detached, to try their luck in the trading activities. It was due to the fact that the trade activities helped to gain economic prominence and earn wealth. The requirement of money was a very basic need for sustaining self and to buy bullocks. As bullocks were most essential for the *tanda* to continue the transportation activities and indirectly to generate wealth.

A famous Rajasthani proverb clearly highlights the importance of bullock trade. It says '*Kheti motha ri; vyapar balda ro*'; it means that in the arid areas only two activities help to earn livelihood, i.e. the cultivation of *moth* (a type of pulse) and business in oxen trading! The Banjaras have attached firmly to the later.

NOTES

1. Denzil Ibbetson, *Panjab Castes*, B.R. Publishing Corporation, Delhi, rpt. 1974, p. 254; and H.A. Rose, *Glossary of the Tribes and Castes of the Punjab and North-West Frontier Province*, Amar Prakashan, Delhi, 1980, pp. 62-3 (hereafter *Glossary of the Tribes and Castes*).
2. Henry M. Elliot, *Memoires on the History, Folklore and Distribution of the Races of the North-Western Provinces of India,* ed. John Beames, Trubner & Co. and Paternoster Row, London, vol. I, 1869, p. 52.
3. Ibid.
4. Rose, *Glossary of the Tribes and Castes*, op. cit., p. 62.
5. Ziauddin Barani, *Tarikh-i-Firuz-Shahi*, ed. Saiyid Ahmed Khan, Bid. I, n.d., Calcutta, 1862, pp. 305-7. Cf. Irfan Habib, 'Merchant Communities', *The Rise of Merchant Empires c. 1350-1750*, Cambridge University Press, Cambridge, 1990, p. 5.
6. William Irvine, *The Army of the Indian Moghuls: Its Organisation and Administration*, Low Price Publication, Delhi, 2004 (rpt.), p. 192.
7. Jean Baptiste Tavernier, *Travels of India*, T.V. Ball, 2nd edn., revised by W.Crooke, London, vol. I, pp. 33, 35. Irfan Habib suggests that the name is misprinted in his text as 'manaris'. The traveller is talking of the carriers. For further reference see, Habib, 'Merchant Communities', op. cit., p. 7.
8. Ibbetson, op. cit., p. 255. He says that the *Labans* are

generally called Banjaras in the eastern districts and *Labana* in the whole of Punjab proper.

9. Jagdish Singh Gahlot, *Marwar Census Report, History and Rituals of Western Rajasthan Castes,* 1891, p. 443.
10. Francis Buchanan, *A Journey from Madras Through the Countries of Mysore, Canara and Malabar*, W. Bulmer and Co., London, 1807, vol. I, p. 205.
11. Elliot, op. cit., pp. 53-4.
12. Rose, op. cit., p. 63.
13. Elliot, op. cit., pp. 52-4.
14. Ibid. (i) Turkias are divided into 36 tribes namely, Tumar, Chauhan, Gahlot, Dilwari, Alwi, Kanoti, Burki, Durki, Shaikh, Nathamir, Aghwan, Badan, Chakiraha, Bahrari, Padar, Kanik, Ghari, Chandual, Teli, Charkhi, Dhangaia, Dhanhikai, Gaddi, Gotahni, Titar, Hindia, Raha, Marquthia, Khakhara, Kareya, Bahlim, Bhatti, Bhandwari, Bargadda, Alia and Khilji.

    (ii) Bayd Banjaras are classified as Jhaloi, Tandar, Hatar, Kapahi, Dandeari, Kachni, Turin, Dhorpahi, Kiri and Bahlim.

    (iii) Labanas are divided into 11 gotras and they joined the Banjara community during Aurangzeb's reign and are natives of Ranthambor.

    (iv) Mukeri sub-groups are reflection of mixed Hindu and Muslim names. Namely the sub-groups are Aghwan, Moghal, Khokhara, Chauhan, Simli-Chauhan, Chothya-Chauhan, Panjtakya-Chauhan, Tauhar, Katherya, Pathan, Tarin-Pathan, Ghori, Ghoriwal, Bangaroa, Kanthya and Bahlim.

    (v) Bahrup Banjaras are classified as tribes of Rathore, Chauhan, Kurri, Powar, Tumar and Bartia.

    (vi) Rathor Banjaras are divided in four sub-groups namely Muchhari, Bahuki, Murhawat and Panot. These groups are further sub-divided like Muchhari who have 52 divisions. Bhuki are divided into 27 groups, Murhawat are classified in 56 groups and Panots have 23 groups. Similarly the other popular groups in Banjaras are Chauhans having 52 *gots*. Pawars having 20 *gots*, Tumar, Tuar and Toris have 52 *gots*. Bartia group claims to have 52 *gots*. Over all, it is visible that these *gots* are a mix of various communities and groups who were joining the Banjaras leaving their own communities but were consciously continuing the names of their clans inorder to specify and highlight their genelogical connections.

15. Tavernier, op. cit., pp. 33-4.
16. Gahlot, op. cit., p. 444.
17. Rose, op. cit., p. 63.
18. R.V. Russell and Rai Bahadur Hira Lal, *Tribes and Castes of the Central Provinces of India*, MacMillan, London, 1916, vol. III, p. 170.
19. Ibid., p. 171.
20. See *Dastur Komwar-Charan*, vol. 7, pp. 573-658. The record containing information on the protocol of Jaipur state is named as *Dastur Komwar* which means (rules applying to people). These records are state maintained entries comprising of 32 volumes, these *dasturs* cover mainly the years from AD 1718-1918. All these volumes are preserved in Rajasthan State Archives at Bikaner.
21. C.A. Bayly, *Rulers, Townsmen and Bazaars: North Indian Society in the Age of British Expansion c. 1770-1870*, Cambridge University Press, Cambridge, 1983.
22. Muzaffar Alam, 'Sikh Uprisings under Banda Bahadur, 1708-1715', *Studies in History*, vol. XLI, no. 2, 1979, pp. 210-11.
23. See W. Crooke, *The Tribes and Castes of N.W. India*, Cosmo Publications, Delhi, 1974 (rpt.), pp. 150-1 and 154-5.

24. R.V. Russell and R.B. Hira Lal, *Tribes and Castes of the Central Provinces of India,* vol. II, Macmillan, London, 1916, p. 178.
25. Ibid., p. 178.
26. Ibbetson, op. cit., p. 254.
27. Russell and Lal, *Tribes and Castes of Central Provinces of India*, op. cit., p. 172.
28. Ibid., pp. 171-2.
29. Elliot, op. cit., pp. 32-3.
30. Ibid., p. 33-7; Gahlot, op. cit., p. 443.
31. For details see Appendix III. This is initial reporting of the monument. Research needs to be carried forward to explore its full significance.
32. The names are Badami, Nilofor, Ruksana, Gulab, Chawali, Rama, etc.
33. Russell and Lal, op. cit., pp. 173-9.
34. Ibid., pp. 175-6.
35. Tavernier, op. cit., p. 35.
36. Russell and Lal, op. cit., pp. 176-8.
37. Gahlot, op. cit., p. 445.
38. All these are popular local deities in Rajasthan. Many temples in villages can be seen of these deities, where the villagers visit and make offerings for protection of their animal wealth. This type of structure (see Plate 6) in temple buildings is exclusively dedicated to the minor deities like the ones discussed in text.
39. Most of these folk-heroes are worshipped as deities – Tejaji, Gugaji, Pabuji, Ramdevji, etc., existed between AD 1100 and 1500. See John D. Smith, *The Epic of Pabuji: A Study of Transcription and Translation*, Katha Books, New Delhi, 1991, pp. 6-7; and Dominique-Sila Khan, *Conversion and Shifting Identity: Ramdev Pir and Ismailies in Rajasthan*, Manohar, Delhi, 2003, pp. 68-9.
40. Shirley Trembath, 'The Rani Bhatiyani Songs: New or

Recycled Material', in N. Singhi and Rajender Joshi (eds.), *Religion, Rituals & Royalty*, Rawat Publication, Jaipur, 1999, pp. 214-26.

41. Dominique-Sila Khan, op. cit., p. 65.
42. Russell and Lal, op. cit., pp. 176-7.
43. Ibid., pp. 177-8.
44. Ibid., pp. 178-82.
45. Ibid., pp. 173-5.
46. Ibid., p. 175.
47. Elliot, op. cit., p. 56.
48. Ibid., p. 56.
49. Russell and Lal, op. cit., pp. 182-3.
50. Ibid., pp. 183-4.
51. Manisha Choudhary, 'Migrating Banjaras and Settling Tandas: An Un-noticed Contribution', *International Journal of History and Cultural Studies*, vol. 3, Issue 4, 2017, DOI: http://dx.doi.org/10.20431/2454-7654.0304003, pp. 26-35. A research paper presented at International Seminar on theme of 'Migration and Settlement: Development of Cross-Cultural India' held at Jodhpur on 25-6 July 2017.
52. See Plates 3, 4, 7 and 9.
53. Much of the information regarding their dressing pattern and use of jewellery is based on personal interviews with Banjara leaders and other members of a Banjara *carvan* camping at Sikar (Rajasthan). I personally interviewed them on 25-8 May, 10-12 July, 18 October and 25-9 December 2008, and 8 January 2016. The raised *dupatta* in cone shape on the head is with the help of *chund*. Necessarily it is kept covered. See Plates 4 and 7.
54. See Plates 3, 4 and 7.
55. See Plates 3, 8 and 11.
56. See Plate 11.

CHAPTER TWO

The Banjaras as Transporters

THE WORD BANJARA denotes a community which covers various persons from varied classes and castes. Thus, the common appellation of Banjara has been applied to a rather heterogeneous group of people. It may be suggested that the demographic expansion of the Banjaras may have also been caused by a process of social amalgation of various tribes that were making the transition from mobile pastoralism to transporters in various parts of India. 'Banjara' became a identity marker of newly emerging nomadic community of grain transporters. The name Banjara, is most probably derived from the Sanskrit word *Vanij* which is also a source of nomenclature for the Indian mercantile caste of Bania.[1]

In the sources of Delhi Sultanate, the term Banjara is not mentioned. When Alauddin Khilji employed some transporters to bring grain from the villages, these people had been given the name of *karavanis.* These *karavanis* were put in chains until they agreed to abide by the diktats of the Sultan.[2] Clearly, the use of the term Banjara appears to be a later development.

The Banjaras were the transporters who moved in large *carvans* or *tandas* carrying the goods on the back of their bullocks. They lived a joyous life in camps. The movement of a *tanda*, is like a single unit operating under the leadership of *carvan* leaders called *Nayak*. Each Banjara troop has a *Nayak*, whom all implicitly obey and trust in all matters connected with their traditions and conduct.[3] The term appears to have been derived from a Sanskrit word *Nayaka* / *Naik*, which means a chief. Other Banjaras are not addressed by this title.[4] *Naik* is also a Telugu word meaning 'lord' or master.[5]

As the office of *Nayak* is not hereditary his selection as *Nayak* depends on the consent of the community. The suffix of *Nayak* was added to the name of the leader.[6] The religion of a person was never the basis for choosing a Banjara *Nayak*.[7] Anyone, irrespective of his religion could be chosen as a *Nayak* but only from the larger community (troop) of the Banjaras.

The Banjaras as transporters evolved in the medieval centuries with the expansion of empires and the growth of services; especially military as well as civil, at the centre and provincial level. Heavy expenditure of the state necessitated to impose more fiscal demand on the peasants. The collection of revenue in kind entailed huge movement of grain from the countryside to the cities. The Banjaras were deployed as transporters due to their reliability and efficiency. Thus, the involvement of Banjaras in the form of large *carvans* moving things from place to place injected a lot of life into the internal trade of medieval India.

The Banjaras are owners of pack-bullocks. Oxen were used as means of transportation.[8] The ox as a means of transportation was preferred over other animals like camel used by the Rebaris and horses employed by merchants of Arabia and Persia. The landscape of the Indian subcontinent is very suitable for the movement of oxen. The pack-oxen were preferred over the bullock cart as the former was swift and cheaper as compared to the latter. For example, whenever the season for overseas voyages pressed and the merchants wished to get the goods quickly to

Surat for further shipment, they loaded them on oxen and not on carts.[9] For arranging transportation of goods in bulk the Banjaras bought and sold oxen in large number. Moreover, the Banjaras used to replenish their stock of oxen if emergency so required. For example, in AD 1716, the Banjaras bought 21 oxen by paying a high amount to the villagers of *pargana* Tonk.[10]

Besides speed, swiftness and convenience the other factors which contributed to the employment of oxen was the ability of the animal to carry enough weight. Needless to say, that the necessity of transporting goods in bulk made the Banjaras indispensable. A bullock could travel quite fast and it would normally be less expensive than a cart. The pack-oxen travelled slowly, grazing while they were moving in herds[11] and no one forbid them from grazing the oxen.[12] All this reduced the cost of feeding, watching and guiding them. Consequently, the expanse of transport was greatly reduced thereby making it the cheapest possible means of transporting goods.[13]

Such a mode of grain carriage made them to adopt a semi-nomadic lifestyle. The Banjaras not only brought grains to the city but also controlled the process of selling and buying in markets. Though, the Banjara presence was quite pervasive in north India, they were also present in other parts of the subcontinent.[14] These Banjara traders were known by different names in different places but all of them undertook the same job of transporting and trading.

B.R. Grover points out that the groups of adjacent villages depended on the local *mandis* both for commercial crop and non-agricultural products. The *katra* and *mahal* of a *pargana* invariably served as a link between the villages and *qasbas*.[15]

The commercial centres were known as *mandis* where the agricultural and non-agricultural surplus was sold for further export to the cities. On the other hand these marketing centres also catered to the need of the villagers by providing those goods which were not available locally. The *mandi* imported these goods from other cities. The *mandis* were controlled by the mercantile communities who maintained detailed and daily record of the sale and purchase. The mercantile communities kept control over the supply of goods from the *qasbas* to the cities. These mercantile organizations were recognized by the state to deal in specific goods. Thus, they regulated the trade and upshot the direction of the production process for the regions. They had regular contracts with the

Banjaras who helped to maintain the internal and external trade by carrying goods from one place to another.[16] The Banjaras did not have direct link with the villages or the primary producers. They usually collected grains from the local officials who were entitled to collect revenue in kind from the villages and subsequently, sell the collection to the Banjaras. Thus, the local officials were a critical link between the Banjaras and *qasba* markets. If the Banjaras refused to collect the grain from the official granaries, the local officials had the authority to penalize them.[17] Many a times, the zamindars also forced sale of grain if it was not purchased voluntarily by the Banjaras.

At times the Banjaras refused to come and buy grains. Various factors were responsible for keeping the Banjaras away for a long time. Whenever the fights in a *mandi* amongst the weighman, seller and purchaser became intense, the Banjaras avoided going to such *mandis.*[18] There are many cases reported in our sources about the reluctance of the Banjaras to visit some *qasbas* of eastern Rajasthan during the seventeenth century. In the official records we have come across some factors responsible for the non-arrival of the Banjaras. In second half of the seventeenth century and early eighteenth century the disturbances caused by the *Bhomia* revolts which rendered the trade routes unsafe was one of the main reasons for the non-arrival of the Banjaras.[19] The imposition of excessive *rahdari* (transit cess) also dissuaded the Banjaras from visiting the region. All these factors put together halted the movement of the Banjaras, thereby causing a temporary set-back to the internal trade of goods in the region. The reasons for the non-arrival of the Banjaras for collection of grain,[20] were sought to be resolved/erased by the state; therefore, the armies were sent to punish the rebellious *Bhomias* and local officials were instructed not to demand excessive *rahdari*.[21]

The non-collection of grains by the Banjaras from the state granaries were immediately reported to the ruler.[22] *Faujdars* were ordered to provide security to the Banjaras in order to restore their movement on the routes.[23] The local officials who themselves were clandestinely engaged in grain trade also persuaded the concerned authorities to reduce the taxes and duties on the Banjaras in order to provide incentive to them to resume buying.[24]

Despite their herculean efforts, the local officials often failed to attract the Banjaras. At last, attempts were made by them to send some wise men to bring the Banjaras to the *mandis* (*syana admi Banjara ne manawa ne bhejya chhe*). Very often the Banjaras were given *paagh* (a turban) as a mark of honour so that they could collect the grain or salt.[25] As the Banjaras had become the sole channel for disposing of its collected revenue, the state had to look after their well being.

The pattern of commercial life in any area was governed by the geographical settings, the commercial importance of the region and the needs of the population residing therein. Though the Banjaras have been in contact with the merchants, they were not transporters of merchant's goods alone. They also acted as suppliers of army, transporters of grains, salt, butter, ghee and various other things which were in abundance at some places but scarcely available at other places travelled by them. This not only helped them in making money but also made them inordinately relevant for a large segment of the population.

The following observation of Peter Mundy while travelling from Agra to Puttana clearly highlights the social and economic importance of the Banjaras:

They are sometimes hired merchants, but most commonly they are the merchants themselves, buying of grain where it is cheap to be had, and carrying it to place where it is dearer and from thence again relate themselves with any thing that will yield benefit in other places, as salt, sugar, butter etc.[26]

Though the Banjaras traded in a number of commodities, they were major suppliers of food grains. For their service the Banjaras charged a transportation fee. The cost of transportation was quite high. Goods from one place to another were taken in *kafilas* (*carvans*) by the Banjaras who maintained supplies of goods between different parts of the country and also to the sea ports of India for further export to other countries.[27]

The organization of land transport which was not free of troubles was largely controlled and organized by the Banjaras. The Banjaras operated both on short and long distance routes. Interesting observations made by different persons about the Banjara trade indicate a kind of specialization in various types of commodities by each *carvan*. Accordingly, they specialized in carrying salt,[28] food grains,[29] butter,[30] sugar, pepper, turmeric,[31] betel-nut, cotton[32] and saltpetre especially during the seventeenth century. William Crooke adds up brassware and iron to the list of items that were transported by the Banjaras.

Salt was the most heavily supplied commodity by the Banjaras from Rajasthan. It might be due to the absence of any other salt producing area in north India.

For instance in AD 1666 nearly 6,500 *mann* (40 *sers* = 1 *mann*) salt was sold to Banjaras in a single deal.[33] A wholesale salt market was established in the city of Jaipur. It is still present and is popularly known as the *Lun Mandi.* The Sambhar lake in Jaipur is India's largest inland salt lake and is the largest salt production unit in India, since ancient times. The Banjaras were to make all their salt purchases from Jaipur rather than directly from Sambhar where salt was manufactured.[34] Salt production was not a widely undertaken activity in other parts of north India and it was an essential commodity of day to day use. Therefore, a constant demand for it was always present. Besides it large quantity of salt was also required in the textile industries for dyeing. This clearly indicates that the Jaipur state use to make huge profits by selling salt to the Banjaras. Salt was not only manufactured at Sambhar lake but in many other parganas of Jaipur state.

The Banjaras were not only the suppliers of grain they also acted as suppliers to the armies. This is described in some details by Emperor Jahangir in his autobiography:

> As there was little cultivation between Multan and Qandahar, the despatch of a large army without provisions was not to be thought of. It was therefore decided to encourage the grain-sellers who in the language of India are called Banjara, and, providing them with money, to take them along with the victorious army, so that there might be no difficulty about supplies. The Banjaras are a tribe. Some of them have 1,000 bullocks, and some more or less. They take grain from different districts (*bulukat*) into the towns and sell it. They go along with the armies, and with such an army there would be 100,000 bullocks or more.[35]

The large number of oxen mentioned by Emperor Jahangir does not appear to be an exaggeration. The Banjaras kept large number of oxen for carrying the trade, as the increased number of oxen helped the *tanda* to transport a raised quantity of goods on the back of each ox. According to Tavernier each ox carried a load weighing 300 or 350 livers.[36]

However, Peter Mundy says that: 'Each oxen, one with another carrying four great maunds, each maund near 16 gallons is 112,000 bushells London measures.'[37] As one gallon is equal to 3.79 kg weight.

Therefore, weight of one maund is 60.57 kg (upto 2 decimal points). So, the 4 maunds on each ox which is around 16 gallons will amount to 969.12 kg. Hence, each ox on an average was carrying a load of 1,000 kg. This certifies the load carrying capacity of the animal. The travel accounts and memoirs also inform us about the distance travelled by an ox each day. There are variations in our sources about the distance travelled by an ox per day. Peter Mundy's, travel account puts that at the most they travelled 6 or 7 miles a day.[38] Francis Buchanan says that: 'They travelled daily at the rate of 3 computed cosses, which may be about 12 British miles and they took 3 hours to perform this journey'.[39] In the memoirs of Russell and Elliot, we get a lot of information about the communities, castes and tribes, but nothing about the quantum of trade carried by Banjaras and the miles travelled by their bullocks in a day. The relative absence of trade details in the memoirs of Russell and Elliot could be attributed to the fascination felt by them towards the well organized colourful *carvans* of Banjaras. Might be due to it they wrote extensively on the advents, the social and cultural organization of the Banjaras and, the economic worth of their activity was missed. Somehow, the various dimensions of the Banjara trade didn't hit the keen observers and escaped both their notice and notes.

The Banjaras owned large number of oxen. Each *tanda* had nearly 1,000 to 12,000 oxen. Tavernier gives an astonishing figure of 10,000 to 12,000 oxen in a *tanda*.[40] Travelling in India, Peter Mundy encountered a *tanda* of Banjaras consisting of 14,000 oxen all laden with grain. Again on 25 August 1632, he went past by another *tanda* of oxen, numbering 20,000 laden with sugar.[41] Taking from Lt. Col. Fitzclarence's notes; Irvine records, 'have seen them with droves of 50,000 bullocks'.[42] The large number of oxen travelling at a time in a *tanda* subsequently suggests that large quantities of various goods were transported by the Banjaras. The word *tanda* means *carvan*. It is clear from the usage of the word in folklore where the responsibility about the safety of *tanda* is in on each member of the *tanda*.[43] Therefore, the security of *tanda* was a joint exercise for the members of *tanda*. Irvine says that 'Guards with matchlocks and spears are placed at the corners, and their dogs do duty as advanced posts'.[44]

The Banjaras also took responsibility for the security of their respective *carvans* while travelling or halting. This was in addition to the security provided by the state. Accompanied by armed guards the Banjaras also kept dogs of various breeds with their *carvan* for keeping watch.[45] The importance of Banjaras as suppliers of official grain and suppliers to the army enhanced their status. They were provided enroute security on behalf of the state. The zamindars of any region were required to ensure their free passage in their respective zamindari jurisdiction.[46]

Tavernier while writing about the Banjaras who are hired as transporters by the merchants notes that:

> Each wagon is drawn by ten to twelve oxen and accompanied by four soldiers, whom the owner of the merchandise is obliged to pay. Two of them walk on each side of the wagon, over which two ropes are passed, and the four ends are held by soldiers, so that if the wagon threatens to upset in a bad place, the two soldiers who are on the opposite side to hold the ropes right, and prevent its turning over.[47]

The Banjaras acted not only as transporters, grain suppliers and traders, they played a more vital role during the medieval centuries. The Mughal sources clearly indicate that they were also acting as the army suppliers. Such a role of the Banjaras has also been confirmed by British official reports. 'Under the

Afghan and Mughal Empire, they were the commissariat of the imperial forces',[48] observed Denzil Ibbetson. Acknowledging the importance and utility of Banjaras as military suppliers, Emperor Jahangir himself noted in his memoirs that the Banjaras bring grain from the villages to the towns and also accompany armies. This observation was made in connection with the Qandahar campaign.[49] On a particular occasion the Banjaras carried grain and butter to Balaghat and Burhanpur and kept them well stocked so that the large armies of the Mughals stationed in that barren area did not have to experience any scarcity of provisions.[50] The butter and ghee was stored in earthen pots for transportation. The mouth of baked clay pot was covered with cotton cloth. Such innovative novelty for making the transportation effective are unique to Banjaras.

Needless to say that, the importance of Banjaras was immense for both the civil population and military. Keeping it in mind, the state tried to keep the Banjara transporters happy and even honoured them time and again. The chiefs and zamindars often offered robes of honour to Banjara chiefs on their safe arrival in their territories.[51] Russell also confirms the role of Banjaras as suppliers of army and notes that the native powers never concern themselves about providing for their forces, and have no idea of a grain and victualling, which forms so great an object in a European campaign.[52] Further, he notes that the sacred character attained by Banjaras is mainly due to their efficiency as the suppliers of the fighting armies. Highlighting the role of Banjaras as commissariate suppliers, Irvine records that, 'It is by these people that the Indian armies in the field are fed, and they are never injured by either army.'[53] As discussed in earlier chapters the Banjaras were not only visible in north-western India. They were also present in the southern states. The arrival of Banjaras in Deccan is linked by Cumberlege to the Asaf Khan's campaign of Deccan in *c.* 1630.[54]

Throughout the seventeenth and eighteenth centuries the state extended protection to the Banjaras so that the flow of trade remains intact. However, the Banjaras were often reported to be harassed by the local officials over the collection of *rahdari*. Whenever, any act of extortion by any local official was reported, the state settled the case in favour of the Banjaras.[55]

For instance in AD 1721 Gidhva Bohra was

subjected to a penalty of Rs. 10 for harassing Banjaras while they were on their way.[56] In pargana Tonk when Mathura Das Khangarot took excessive *rahdari* from some Banjaras he was penalized for this act.[57] A penalty of Rs. 5 was imposed on Padam Singh Rajawat for realizing an additional *rahdari* of Rs. 3 from a Banjara.[58] A high penalty of Rs. 12 was also realized from an unnamed official who was caught harassing the Banjaras.[59] These favours by the state to the *carvanis* are prominent indicators, that the state sided with the Banjaras due to their vital role in carrying out the economic activities, supply of armies and for keeping the transportation smooth.

The various mishappenings like theft and robbery on routes quite often discouraged the Banjaras from taking up the trade. In such cases the state extended help and provided full protection to the Banjaras. For example the *thanedar* of Dausa imposed a penalty of Rs. 50 on a thief who had stolen the bullock of a Banjara.[60] A penality of Rs. 21 was taken from a *qanungo* who was found harassing the Banjaras.[61] Once, the local officials and *chowkidars* caught a man who organized a theft in a Banjara *carvan* and penalized him with Rs. 5 and 8 *anna* for the act.[62]

The cases of en-route robbery and theft were also reported to the state officials from *mauza* (village) Mehrauli and *mauza* Barwala. The Banjaras were looted for which a penalty of Rs. 25 and 11 was taken respectively from both the villages.[63] If any loss took place on the routes due to the negligence of the Banjaras the state also penalized them for such losses caused due to negligence.

From our sources a clear picture of state support to the Banjara emerges. In many cases of theft and robbery the state could not ignore the interest of the Banjaras. The Banjaras had direct access to report the cases to the ruler, if they were not satisfied by the decisions of local officials.[64] State officials were also warned not to obstruct the traders by demanding excessive *rahdari*.[65] As the Banjaras had become the key element in the network of internal trade, their interest could not be ignored anymore. The keenness shown by the state to redress the grievances of the Banjaras shows the latter's importance in the commercial world of the medieval times.

At times the Banjara *carvans* are also reported to have internal conflicts while travelling on the routes. The fights and petty quarrels amongst the *carvans* were not favourable for the trade because it needed a smooth working. The state also tried to mitigate such conflicts. Narrating an interesting case Tavernier notes in his account:

> The great Mogul, considering that these quarrels were prejudicial to commerce and to the transport of food in his Kingdom, arranged that the chief of the two carvans should come to see him. When they arrived, the king after he had advised them for their mutual benefits, to live for the future in harmony with each other, and not to fight again when they met, presented each of them with a lakh or 100000 rupees and a chain of pearls.[66]

Such bracing importance of the Banjaras was due to their role as indispensable suppliers of goods. Unexpected events such as thefts and internecine conflicts between individual Banjaras and two *carvans* could result in a considerable loss of goods. If due to these occurrences the Banjaras failed to bring the required supplies it could cause great scarcity for the army and general population. In AD 1576, during siege of Kakandah in *suba* Ajmer, Akbar's army is reported to have suffered great scarcity of food grains, because of the non-arrival of Banjaras with their supplies.[67] The role of Banjaras as suppliers of goods to armies was quite immense. It has been described by William Irvin as 'The supplies of grain were brought in on the back of bullock by the wandering dealers known as Banjaras. It is by these people that the Indian Armies in fields are fed, and they are never injured by either army.'[68] The importance of Banjaras for armies is more rigouresly stated during the annexation of Deccan by the Mughal Governor Asaf Khan. To ensure the supplies to his fighting armies in Deccan, Asaf Khan not only employed Bhangi and Jhangi Banjara with 1,80,000 and 52,000 pack-bullocks respectively, but even provided solution to the difficulties faced by both the Banjaras (Bhangi and Jhangi) about the non-availability of grass and water for their cattle.[69] Asaf Khan, provided them a order engraved on a copper sheet in letters made out of gold stating '*Ranjan ka Pani, Chhappar ka ghas, din ke tin khun muaf; Aur jahan Asaf ke ghore, wahan Bhangi Jhangi ke bail*'.[70] This grant is still in possesion of the descendents of Bhangi *Naik*.[71] By the above event the signficance of Banjaras for Mughal armies is well established. The rival armies also persuaded the Banjaras for supplies and this clearly underlines their importance as the transporters for the fighting armies in the battlefields. The Banjaras were not only suppliers of the Mughal army but continued to do so for the British forces as well. The association of

Banjaras with the rebel Sikhs also indicates their association with some rebellious groups active in medieval India. The help of the Banjaras was also taken by British authorities in early years of their settlement in the Indian subcontinent. For example, in AD 1791-2, the Banjaras were employed to supply grains to the British army during the siege of Seringapatam. 'The Duke of Wellington in his Indian campaigns regularly engaged them as part of the commissariat staff of his army.'[72]

Needless to say that, all the polities including the Mughals, the eighteenth century states of Rajasthan[73] and the British authorities had realized the importance of the Banjaras.

Therefore, all these states tried to keep Banjaras happy and contented. The Banjaras were popular and were sought after as trusted and loyal transporters. This quality helped them to lift large quantities of valuable goods. Once when 27 carts carrying grain had not reached Delhi, the *diwan* ordered an *amil* to make a deal with the Banjaras for the transportation of the remaining cargo of wheat and barley.[74] In June 1619, due to shortage of sugar at Surat, the English Resident there had to order his factors at Agra to make contact with Banjaras to procure 100 *mann* of sugar every year and send it to Surat annually.[75] While travelling in central India Travenier notes that 'when the season presses, and they wish to get the goods quickly to Surat, in order to ship them, they load them on oxen and not on carts.'[76]

During the late seventeenth century the Banjaras were transporting less grain due to the fear of rebels in the north-western region of India. The downward trend in their travels had not only shaken the economy, but also forced the authorities to take steps for keeping Banjaras happy.

Thus, it can be said that the evolution of Banjaras as transporters was a unique feature of the medieval Indian economy. The Banjaras were not only transporters they were merchants as well. As transporters the vital role played by them was dual in character. Though, primarily they were suppliers of grains to distant markets, their role as suppliers of armies was equally important. Needless to say that, the Banjaras played the role of transporter 'par excellence' throughout the medieval centuries. In the region of our study the movement of the Banjaras was quite brisk. In the next chapter we will discuss the commodity structure of the trade carried out by the Banjaras.

NOTES

1. Henry M. Elliot, *Memoirs on the History, Folk-lore and Distribution of the Races of the North-Western Provinces of India*, vol. I, Trubner & Co., London, 1869, p. 52.
2. Ziauddin Barani, *Tarikh-i-Firuz-Shahi,* ed. Saiyid Ahmed Khan, Bibliotheca Indica, Calcutta, 1862, pp. 305-7, cf. Irfan Habib, 'Merchant Communities', *The Rise of Merchant Empires c. 1350-1750*, Cambridge University Press, Cambridge, 1990, p. 373.
3. Elliot, op. cit., p. 56.
4. Denzil Ibbetson, *Punjab Castes*, p. 254.
5. R.V. Russell and Rai Bahadur Hira Lal, *Tribes and Castes of the Central Provinces of India*, p. 188.
6. *Arsattha, Pargana* Narayana, dt. VS 1781/AD 1724.

   The name of one such leader is mentioned as Chander Bhan *Nayak* and *Nayak* Haider Mani whereas the names of other members are mentioned with Banjara as suffix along with their names. For furthur information see Appendix II.
7. *Arsattha, Pargana* Lalost, dt. VS 1794/AD 1737.

   The name of the *carvan* leader is Haider Mani *Nayak.*
8. Various sources tell us about the oxen used by Banjara as means of transportation. 'The Banjaras load the oxen called Balad' (Jagdish Gahlot, *Marwar Census Report*, 1891, op. cit., p. 443). 'They carry goods on back of their bullocks' (Jahangir, *Tuzuk-i-Jahangiri,* ed. Saiyid Ahmed, Ghazipur and Aligarh, 1863-4, p. 345). 'They give an ox a load weighing 300 or 350 livers' (Tavernier, *Travels in India*, p. 32). 'They bring the drug hither in small *carvan* of 10-12 oxen' (Francis Buchanan, op. cit., p. 203). 'These people go

dispersely, driving their laden Oxen before them' (Peter Mundy, op. cit., p. 96). 'I have seen them with drovers of 500 bullocks' (R.V. Russell and R.B. Hira Lal, *Tribes and Castes of the Central Provinces of India,* p. 169).

9. Tavernier, op. cit., p. 32.
10. *Arsattha, Pargana* Tonk, dt. VS 1773/AD 1716.
11. Francis Buchanan, *Journey from Madras*, vol. I, p. 206.
12. Peter Mundy, *The Travels of Peter Mundy in Europe and Asia, 1608-1667*, vol. II, *Travels in Asia, 1628-1634*, Col. Sir Richard Carnac Temple, Hakluyt Society, London, 1914, pp. 96-7.
13. Irfan Habib, *The Agrarian System of Mughal India*, Oxford University Press, New Delhi, 1999, p. 69.
14. Banjaras of Bangalore are described by Francis Buchanan (Buchanan, op. cit., p. 203). The Banjaras of Punjab are called *Labanas* (see Ibbetson, op. cit., p. 254). The Banjaras of central India, western India and Gorakhpur are explained by Henry Elliot (Elliot, op. cit., pp. 52-3).
15. B.R. Grover, 'An Integrated Pattern of Commercial Life in Rural Society of North India during the Seventeenth and Eighteenth Centuries', in Sanjay Subrahmanyam (ed.), *Money and the Market in India c. 1100-1700*, Oxford University Press, Delhi, 1998, pp. 222-3.
16. Ibid., p. 222.
17. *Arsattha, Pargana* Narayana, dt. VS 1781/AD 1724. As described in record a penalty of Rs. 8 was imposed on Banjara who denied to purchase the grain.
18. *Arzdasht*, dt. *Mangsir vadi* 5, VS 1740/AD 1683.
19. R.P. Rana, *Rebels to Rulers: The Rise of Jat Power in Medieval India, c. 1665-1735*, Manohar, Delhi, 2006, pp. 142-68.

20. *Amber Record*, written by Ajit Das and Laxmidas from *Pargana* Tonk, dt. *Fagun Sudi*, vs 1723/AD 1666.
21. *Arzdasht* written by *Amil* Nainsukh to Sawai Jai Singh from *Pargana* Sambhri, dt. *Mangsir Sudi* 2, vs 1766/AD 1709. Ibid., dt. *Posh Vadi* 7, vs 1766/AD 1709.
22. *Arzdasht*, written by Than Singh Bhandari, *Amil* from *Pargana* Toda Rai Singhpur to Sawai Jai Singh, dt. *Mangsir Sudi* 12, vs 1766/AD 1709.
23. *Arzdasht*, written by *Amil* Nain Sukh to Sawai Jai Singh from *Pargana* Sambhari, dt. *Mangsir Sudi* 11, vs 1766/AD 1709.
24. *Arzdasht*, written by *Amil* Nain Sukh of *Pargana* Sambhari, dt. *Phagun Vadi* 6, vs 1766/AD 1709.
25. Ibid., dt. *Posh Vadi* 7, vs 1766/AD 1709 *Chitti* from Kotla written by Ajay Raj, dt. *Kati Vadi* 5, vs 1723/AD 1666.
26. Mundy, op. cit., pp. 95-6. Standardized English words have been used instead of the original notings of Mundy.
27. Mundy, op. cit., pp. 95-6; Tavernier, op. cit., pp. 32-3.
28. Tavernier, op. cit., p. 32; Madhavi Bajekal, 'The State and the Rural Grain Market in Eighteenth Century Eastern Rajasthan', *IESHR*, New Delhi, p. 468; Jagdish Singh Gahlot, op. cit., p. 443; Elliot, op. cit., p. 55; Mundy, op. cit., p. 96; W. Crooke, *The North-Western Provinces of India*, 1897, p. 27.

    Arzdasht, written by *Amil* Nain Sukh of *Pargana* Sambhari to Sawai Jai Singh, dt. *Mangsir Sudi* 2, vs 1766/AD 1709.
29. Wheat and Rice are carried. See Mundy, op. cit., p. 95.
30. Mundy, op. cit., p. 95.
31. Elliot, op. cit., p. 55.
32. Buchanan, op. cit., pp. 204-6; Crooke, op. cit., p. 27.

33. *Chitti* of Ajay Raj from Kolta, dt. *Kati Vadi* 5, vs 1723/ AD 1666.
34. Madhavi Bajekal, 'The State and the Rural Grain Market', *IESHR*, p. 468.
35. *Tuzuk-i-Jahangiri*, tr. Alexander Rogers, and ed. Henry Beveridge, vol. 2, Low Price Publication, Delhi, 2006 (rpt.), pp. 233-4.
36. Tavernier, op. cit., p. 32.
37. Mundy, op. cit., pp. 95-8.
38. Ibid., p. 96.
39. Buchanan, op. cit., pp. 204-5.
40. Tavernier, op. cit., pp. 32-3.
41. Mundy, op. cit., pp. 95-8.
42. William Irvine, *The Army of the Indian Mughals: Its Organisation and Administration,* Low Price Publication, Delhi, 2002 (rpt.), p. 192.
43. See folklore on p. 82. The women of *tanda* were entrusted with the watch-keeping duty because the Banjara is tempramentaly bad.
44. William Irvine, *The Army of the Indian Mughals: Its Organisation and Administration,* Low Price Publication, Delhi, 2004 (rpt.), p. 192.
45. Russell and Lal, op. cit., pp. 188-90. The various breeds of dogs specially hounds are kept in the *tanda*. I have seen them during my visits to the *tandas*.
46. Grover, op. cit., p. 238.
47. Tavernier, op. cit., pp. 34-5.
48. Ibbetson, op. cit., p. 254.
49. *Tuzuk-i-Jahangiri*, op. cit., p. 233-4.
50. Syed Aslam Ali, 'The Role of Banjaras in 17th Century

Trade', unpublished article available in the library of Aligarh Muslim University, Aligarh, p. 8.
51. Grover, op. cit., pp. 238-9.
52. Russell and Lal, op. cit., p. 167.
53. Irvine, *The Army of the Indian Mughals,* p. 192.
54. Russell and Lal, op. cit., p. 168.
55. *Nakal* (copy) *Arzdasht, Pargana* Amber written by Purohit Harsh Ram to Maharaja Jai Singh, dt., *Posh Vadi* vs 1759/ AD 1702.
56. *Arsattha, Pargana* Fagui, dt. vs 1778/AD 1721.
57. *Arsattha, Pargana* Tonk, dt. vs 1779/AD 1722.
58. Ibid.
59. Ibid.
60. *Arsattha, Pargana* Dausa, dt. vs 1769/AD 1712.
61. *Arsattha, Pargana* Tonk, dt. vs 1768/AD 1711.
62. *Arsattha, Pargana* Lalsot, dt. vs 1774/AD 1717.
63. *Arsattha, Pargana* Ao, dt. vs 1751/AD 1694. See Appendix II: entry nos. 47, 48 and 49.
64. *Arzdasht,* written by Sanghi Kalyandas to Ramchand, dt. *Chait Vadi* 13, vs 1719/AD 1662.
65. *Khat* (letter), written by Jait Singh Kamdar, dt. *Fagun Sudi* 15, vs 1766/AD 1709.
66. Tavernier, op. cit., pp. 32-3.
67. Syed Aslam Ali, op. cit., pp. 9-10.
68. Irvin, *The Army of Indian Mughals,* p. 192.
69. Russell and Lal, op. cit., p. 169.
70. Ibid., p. 169. The meaning of couplet goes like this 'If you do not find water elsewhere you may even take it from the pots of my followers; grass you may take from roofs of their huts; and I will pardon you upto three murders a day,

provided that wherever I find my cavalry, Bhangi and Jhangi bullocks shall be with them.'

71. Ibid., p. 169.
72. Russell and Lal, op. cit., p.170.
73. *Arzdasht* written by Kishor Das Rajawat, dt. *Aasoj Sudi* 2, vs 1751/AD 1694.
74. Bajekal, 'The State and Grain Market', op. cit., p. 468.
75. *Factories, 1618-21*, p. 102.
76. Travenier, op. cit., pp. 32-3.

CHAPTER THREE

The Commodity Structure of Banjara Trade

ANALYSING THE EXTENT and organization of the agricultural produce market would help us to determine the magnitude of trade in the sector. The production of vast variety of high value (*jins-i-ala*) as well as low priced crop was a striking feature of Mughal agriculture. As the extent of cultivation was expanding, the total output was also increasing. The agricultural production was subjected to taxation both in kind (*batai*) and cash (*zabt*). In the region of our study, the collection of revenue in kind was widespread.[1] This practice enabled the state to mop up huge quantities of grain from the countryside. The movement of grain from the village to the *qasbas* and from *qasbas* to the cities was a constant feature of the economy of seventeenth and eighteenth centuries.

The extensive trade in food grains from one region to another indicates the existence of surplus and deficit areas in medieval India. It contradicts theories which postulate uniform pattern of self-sufficiency for the entire subcontinent.[2] Tapan Raychaudhuri has discussed in great detail about the areas, where production was surplus and how the surplus produce was made to reach the deficit zones. The organization and working of markets in our region clearly shows that the entire surpluses taken by the state from the peasants were never consumed locally.[3] It had to be transported to distant markets. The *mahajan* who was a moneylender as well a trader played an important role in purchasing the revenue (grain) in kind, either taking it to the nearest market or to the state granary (*awar*).[4]

The collected grain in the form of revenue was put up for sale, i.e. *bichoti*. For the arrangements of sale, the authorities and local officials used various agencies of *vyoparis, banias* and *mahajans* who subsequently handed over the grain to the Banjaras for supply and sale in distant markets. A *chitthi* written by three traders of Dadri in AD 1666 stated that the banias have been engaged for the sale of grains collected as revenue from the *rabi* season. Nearly 5,000 *manns* of grain was sold to them. The sold grains comprised gram (*chana*) and barley (*jau*) and sold at the rate of Rs. 2-8 *anna* and Rs. 2-5 *anna* per *mann* respectively.[5]

In a document dated AD 1684, it is recorded that local officials were persuading the *vyoparis* to buy the grains collected in the form of revenue. The official expressed their satisfaction on the fact that the *mahajan* of the *qasba* and pargana were offering better prices.[6] According to another document *sanghi* Roopchand is reported to have sold grain amounting to Rs. 35,000 to five *mahajans* of Kaladehra. Here it may be mentioned that, in the market of Kaladehra four times more merchants traded as compared to the market of Sambhari. The market of Kaladehra was a nodal point for the disposal of state grains. In AD 1686, it was reported that grains worth Rs. 1,00,000 was lying in the markets of *qasba* Sanganeri. However, the state official managed to sell grains worth Rs. 40,000 out of the above mentioned total.[7]

Thus, looking at various sources, we can say that the sale of grain in the *qasbas* and parganas was mainly controlled by the *banias* and *mahajans*. The *mahajans* and *banias* played a prominent role as the buyers of grain. As these traders could not dispose off such a huge quantity of grain locally, they had to take it to distant markets which normally assured large profits to them. For the transportation of these large quantities of food grains, they had to depend on the Banjaras.

The limitations of long-distance trading in medieval centuries were set by the nature of the means of transport. The transport on land routes was mainly organized by the Banjaras. They were spotted moving in large numbers by various authorities in medieval times. The Banjaras themselves were nomads and they lived with their families in *tandas* which was an organized moving *carvan*. A large *tanda* might contain as many as 600 or 700 souls and upto 12,000-15,000 or even 20,000 bullocks which would have carried about 1,600 to 2,700 tons of goods at a time. On certain occasions such as when a large army had to be supplied, the Banjaras might collect 1,00,000 bullock or more.[8] Peter Mundy on his journey from Surat to Agra found thousands of bullocks carrying food to the imperial camp at Burhanpur while others were returning unladen to carry back more. Similar was the observation of William Irvine who saw

50,000 bullocks in a *tanda*. This indicates to the capacity and better management of Banjara *tanda* who were capable to deal with the sudden increase in the demand and supply of goods.

While walking along the routes, the Banjaras never carried fodder for their animals. The animals were fed directly from the en-route grounds and routes. Irvine notes that 'their cattle are allowed to graze as they proceed on the march'.[9] The direct feeding from the soil further reduced their speed. The bullocks travelled 5-6 miles a day. A close look at the commodity structure of the Banjara trade reveals that their trade was never in perishable items like fruits, vegetables, etc. It was a normal feature of the Banjara trade that after a minimum travel of 3 to 5 days, they made some sale and un-load their bullocks. Most of the commodities carried on the pack-oxen were foodstuff such as rice, wheat, pulses, salt, sugar, butter, ghee, etc., which didn't spoil soon. The major share of trade was mainly in dry items. For example, from *pargana* Chatsu in AD 1712 Banjaras carried rice, *tel*, *gur*, *khand*, sugar, *kirana* and salt. The Banjaras carried grains and salt in bulk.[10] We don't have any evidence to know the rates charged by the Banjaras for transportation. But it must have been cheaper if it excluded the task of security of the *carvan*. While travelling, much of the cost was incurred on guarding the *carvan* and its goods. When the state provided security the charges were less, if the security risk was the responsibility of the Banjaras, the cost of transportation went very high.

During the seventeenth and eighteenth centuries trade was conducted in a number of commodities. But agricultural goods and salt occupied a dominant position. The trading commodities included birds, animals and various articles of amusement like *chimta, khartal, dhup, dholki*, dried skins for making and covering the musical instruments and the items of daily consumption. B.R. Grover's detailed study of the eighteenth century commercial life throws some light on the commodities of trade and the castes of those who carried out trade in particular items like birds, liquor and animals, etc.[11] An insight into the commercial life and the patterns of trade during seventeenth and eighteenth centuries tells us about the multiplicity and magnitude of goods and luxury items produced in India.[12] The Mughal state provided protection to trade and commerce. The facilities provided for enhancement of trade were immense such as minting of coins, standardization of currency, safety of trade routes, facilities on the trade routes and decentralization of the trade. The local merchants of the native areas were free to organize the trading activities in their respective trade zones. The mughal officials were only to regulate and facilitate the trade activities. The imperial officers adopted a conciliatory attitude towards merchants and artisans. Severe penalties were imposed on those who harassed traders. Special facilities were provided to the traders for expediting trade and commerce. In medieval times revenue collection, its disposal, trade and markets were inextricably interconnected. For the smooth working of this system it was necessary that the authorities levied fixed duties on traders.

Trade in the Mughal India was helped by an elaborate system of short-term credit, based on drawing and discounting of the *hundis*. The *hundi* was a written order (promise) to pay an amount, at sight or after a period of time as specified in paper. If anyone wanted to remit money to some other place, he approached a *sarraf* who accepted the amount and wrote a *hundi* to be drawn on his agent. The *sarraf* used to charge for this service.[13] In this commercial world the Banjaras served as an unbroken stream of suppliers to different parts of the country and also to the seaports for export.[14] Thus, the Banjaras were a critical link between the hinterland's centres of production of goods such as textiles, indigo, metal-ware, ivory-products, silk and many others. The quantum of trade carried out by the Banjaras throughout the year was very large. Irfan Habib said:

> even if an ox carried load only for a third of the year, at six miles a day, the Banjaras should have annually conveyed on their cattle 1-14 million metric tons each over an average of 720 miles – or a total of 821 million tons a year. Even for so large a country as India, this could be a massive volume of goods transported.[15]

I also agree with it looking at the repeated mention in the various sources about the huge volume and quantum of goods transported by Banjaras and the constant affirmation of same by various travellers and merchants. Obviously, the Banjaras transported large quantities of goods before the beginning of the railways.

Though, it is not possible to make firm estimates of the total quantum of trade by the Banjaras in the region and period of our study. However, some estimates collected from the scattered information available in our archival sources, indicates to the lifting of huge quantity of grains from the said markets. The quantity of grain to be lifted by the Banjaras from different *qasba* markets has been mentioned in some documents. For example, a report of AD 1662 shows large quantities of grains heaped in the markets of five parganas. The arrival of Banjaras was eagerly awaited by local officials for lifting nearly 90,022 *mann* of grains stored in the following parganas:[16]

S.No.	Pargana	Quantity of grain
1.	Malpura	17,208 *mann*
2.	Niwai	41,001 *mann*
3.	Chatsu	14,535 *mann*
4.	Malarana	10,913 *mann*
5.	Nainwai	63,65 *mann*
Total		90,022 *mann*

The apparent glut of grain in the markets of different parganas was due to the delay in the arrival of Banjaras for collection of the goods. Our evidence shows that Banjaras were postponing their arrival because of *bhomia* (zamindar) unrest which had caused disturbances on the trade routes. Though, the nature of grains are not mentioned in the document. But considering the fact that the sale deed was to be executed after the *rabi* harvest, we may assume that wheat constituted the bulk of the above mentioned total grains. In another document, belonging to *pargana* Rewari the variety of grain has been mentioned. Out of the total amount of 87,640 *mann*, the break up goes like this 38,816 *mann bajra*; 37,769 *mann moth* (a pulse); 3,466 *mann mung* (green gram); 7,032 *mann jawari* (millet); 100 *mann urad* (black gram); 84 *mann til* (sesame seed) and 360 *mann kapas* (cotton).[17] The break up of different types of grains clearly indicates that these had been collected from the *kharif* season. The *amil* of *pargana* Rewari while writing to the *diwan* of Jaipur state expressed his concern about the non-arrival of Banjaras for lifting such a huge quantity of grains. Yet according to another report about 6,000 *mann* of grain was lifted by the Banjaras in AD 1665 for further transport to Jahanabad (Delhi).[18] In AD 1683 two Banjaras, namely, Asogmal and Achgory were reported to be passing through *qasba* Rini (*pargana* Bahatri) carrying 10,000 bundles (*pout*) on the back of their bullocks.[19] In the same report it is further mentioned that these Banjaras were attacked by some retainers of a *bhomia*. In the ensuing skirmish one Banjara was killed and ten men of the *bhomias* were injured. The local *faujadar* imposed a penalty of Rs. 775 on the Banjaras and the *bhomia* went scot free. Such a severe penalty on the Banjaras appears to be unusual. Might it was an effort by the state to discipline the actors and factors of the kingdom. Normally, the state used to favour the Banjaras in such disputes. Needless to say that such a discriminatory behaviour on the part of local officials might have discouraged the Banjaras to visit the region.[20] Non-arrival of the Banjaras made the local officials jittery. Soon the higher authorities sent strict instructions to the pargana officials for creating a conducive atmosphere for the visits of the Banjaras.

The commodity structure of trade practiced by the Banjaras suggests that they were trading mainly in food grains like wheat,[21] rice,[22] millet[23] and the other non-perishable goods like sugar,[24] salt,[25] saltpetre,[26] butter,[27] ghee and pulses. In the year AD 1665, the Jaipur state sold nearly 1,15,000 *mann* of salt for Rs. 11,950 to the Banjaras.[28] The large quantity of salt was sent from Sambhari which was popular for salt manufacturing. Apart from Sambhar there were also many other centres of salt production in the Jaipur state. According to Syed Aslam Ali, the Banjaras transported goods under two systems of security.[29] First, they simply hired out their beasts of burden and carried merchandise on the risk of the owner himself. Under this condition the owner of the merchandise was solely responsible to make arrangements for the safety of the goods during journey upto the destination. He also had to pay road dues, if any. Secondly, the Banjaras took upon themselves whole responsibility of safe delivery of goods at the appointed place. They were to pay all the road dues themselves. The owner was not concerned with the loss of his goods on the way. His only concern was to get his merchandise at the appointed or destined place of delivery.

In AD 1686, Tek Chand the *amil* of *pargana* Dausa reported to the Jaipur *darbar* that about 87,239 *mann* of grain was lying at the pargana *mandi*. This glut had been caused due to the non-arrival of the traders for collecting grain. The sale was also affected due to the harassment of the traders at the *chowkis* (check-posts) on account of *rahdari*. Such harassments usually kept the traders away from the *mandis*.[30]

The mid-nineteenth century poem of Nazir Akbarabadi, titled 'Banjara', provides a long list of commodities that were traded by the Banjaras. The goods were wheat, rice, *moth* (pulses), peas, sugar, *mishri*, *khand*, *giri* (almond), *sambhar* (salt), *dakh* (a spice), *munakka* (big dried grape raisins), *sonth* (a spice), *mirch* (chilli), *kesar* (saffron), *laung* (cloves), *supari* (areca nut), etc. The variety of goods were supplied by the Banjaras who moved in all directions in large *carvans*.[31] While moving in the *carvan*, members themselves used many things out of the above goods.

The elaborate trade system and extended supply of goods made the Banjaras very efficient in maintaining the complex accounts. The Banjaras were illiterate and they didn't have any formal training of account keeping in their community. However, they were familiar with the system of accountancy, due to its use in everyday forms of trading. This practice among the Banjaras was also noted by the British officials. John Malcolm (AD 1824) noted that the Banjaras often engaged in great speculations on their own account. Though being illiterate very few kept written accounts. This habit had made them very acute in memorizing numbers. They had a sharp memory which enabled them to retain the minutest particulars of their extended transactions.[32] 'A Banjara who can read and write is unknown. But their memories, from cultivations are marvelous and very retentive. They carry in their heads, without slip of a mistake, the most varied and complicated transactions and the share of each in such striking a debtor and creditor account as accurately as the best kept ledger, while their history and songs are all learned by heart and transmitted orally from generation to generations',[33] observed Mackenzie. The cases related to the payment of previous dues (*baqaya*) by the Banjaras after their return journey evidently suggests that they did keep some written records. In one such case a Banjara paid Rs. 8 as arrears of some previous penalty.[34] Apart from such occasional references, we do not know anything about their system of accounting. The vast variety and huge quantum of goods supplied by Banjaras definately required proper entries. So, that the goods and quantity of item to be delivered and to be collected consequently shall not get topsy-turvy.

While travelling, the large *carvans* met on different routes moving from Agra, Bengal, Sindh, Rajputana, Gujarat, Malwa, Central India and the Deccan. Noting on the commodity structure of trade carried out by Banjaras, Syed Aslam Ali writes:

> Agra being the capital of the empire was the main centre of business for the Banjaras, where great volume of wheat, rice, sugar and butter brought by them from fertile regions, particularly from the eastern parts and Bengal, was dumped to be supplied further to the other parts of the empire. Grain was also supplied by them to Ajmer and Surat in the west and even to Patna in the east. It was also

taken by them from *suba* (province) Malwa to the coastal town of Baroda. They occasionally procured grain and took it to Qandhar. The Banjaras transported sugar and sugar candy to Surat, Ahmadabad and Broach from Agra. As stated earlier these commodities were first bought to Agra from the areas of surplus production. Saltpetre was transported from Patna to the sea port of Surat and other coastal cities. From the sea coasts, the Banjaras returned with salt which had a ready market in the interior towns.[35]

The Banjaras were not only the principal transporters to the Mughals but they also worked as transporters of the British factors. For example due to the shortage of sugar in June 1619 at Surat, the English Resident at Surat had to order his factors at Agra to make contact with the Banjaras to provide 100 *mann* of sugar to Surat every year.[36]

The ups and downs in the movement of the Banjaras could cause fluctuations in the price of goods. Delays in the supply of goods could cause rise in price whereas timely supplies by the Banjaras could keep the prices stable.[37] For example, in AD 1630-2 the Banjaras were busy feeding the armies of Emperor Shah Jahan. Hence, they were not able to supply goods to famine sticken Gujarat. This led to the sale of grain in the markets of Surat at a high rate of

16 *mahmudis* per *mann* in AD 1631. But with the arrival of Banjaras in January 1632, the prices of wheat and rice at Surat fell to 6¼ *mahmudis* per *mann*.[38] The entire episode clearly shows the social significance and economic indispensability of the Banjaras as transporters of goods particularly in the items of daily utilization.

The Banjaras also played an important role in Mughal India's foreign trade. They supplied the export articles to the sea ports for overseas shipment. The unbroken chain of supplies maintained by the Banjaras made foreign trade flourish. The English factory correspondences usually bemoaned the fact that time and again the English factors at coastal towns were unable to buy a commodity for shipment, as the Banjaras for one reason or the other failed to bring the supply in time.[39] Clearly, the Banjaras had also become fulcrum of India's overseas trade.

Their role was recognized by the Mughal emperors who regularly bestowed honours, awards and robes of honour upon the Banjaras. Having considered their support in the Qandahar campaign as indispensable, Emperor Jahangir rewarded the Banjaras with money to further encourage them to accompany the Imperial army to Qandahar.[40]

Emperor Aurangzeb was more conscious in realizing the economic importance of the Banjaras. He exempted them from paying the grazing fees[41] as well as *rahdari* (i.e. road dues).[42]

Once Mughal Emperor Jahangir favoured two Banjara *Nayaks* with chain of pearls and presented each of them with Rs. 1,00,000 and adviced them of their mutual benefits and took a promise from them that in future they will live in harmony.[43] This might have been done by the emperor to keep the Banjaras happy so that they could continue to supply the goods even during the period when the routes had been rendered unsafe.

In conclusion, it may be said that the Banjaras were the long distance transporters, trading in a wide variety of commodities. They also acted as transport agents of the merchants, Mughal armies and English factors. They were respected and rewarded by the Mughal rulers and Kachhawaha rajas of Jaipur-Amber state as their role in the economy was immense and indispensable. This responsible and respectable position was enjoyed by Banjaras even during the early medieval times where the *carvan* traders (Banjaras) were called *mana purahsara* (people of honour) and were received honourably and treated well.[44] After the decline of the Mughal Empire the successor states continued to use the Banjaras as transporters of goods. The evidences discussed in this chapter clearly indicate that the Jaipur state depended on the Banjaras for the disposal of their grain in distant markets and the armies both of the Mughals and John Company depended on them for the supplies. No wonder the arrival of the Banjaras was eagerly awaited in markets. Despite our inability in determining the total volume of the Banjara trade, its value cannot be underestimated and their significance for the local populace continued to exist.

NOTES

1. S.P. Gupta, *The Agrarian System of Eastern Rajasthan c. 1650-1750*, Manohar, New Delhi, 1986 and Irfan Habib, *The Agrarian System of Mughal India*, Oxford University Press, New Delhi, 1999.
2. Tapan Raychaudhuri, *The Cambridge Economic History of India c. 1200-1750*, vol. I, Orient Longman, Delhi, 1982, p. 330.
3. S.P. Gupta, *The Agrarian System of Eastern Rajasthan c. 1650-1750*, Manohar, New Delhi, 1986.
4. *Chitthi* from Akhay Raj to Diwan Kalyan Das dt. vs 1721/AD 1664, *Chitthi* of Diwan Khushal Chand Kishan Chand, dt. vs 1850/AD 1793.
5. *Chitthi* from Than Singh, Bhawani Shankar Das, Sodan Somachand, dt. *Baishak Vadi* 12, vs 1723/AD 1666.

6. *Arzdasht*, Badri Raj, Jodha Raj, Nathu Ram to Ram Singh, dt. *Chait Sudi* 2, VS 1723/AD 1666.
7. *Arzdasht*, dt. *Asoj Sudi* 10, VS 1743/AD 1686.
8. Habib, *The Agrarian System of Mughal India*, p. 69.
9. Irvine, *The Army of the Indian Mughals*, p. 192.
10. *Dastur-ul Amal, Ghascharai, Pargana* Chatsu, VS 1769/AD 1712.
11. B.R. Grover, 'An Integrated Pattern of Commercial Life in Rural Society of North India during the Seventeenth and Eighteenth Centuries', in Sanjay Subrahmanyam (ed.), *Money and Market in India c. 1100-1700*, Oxford University Press, New Delhi, 1998, pp. 230-1.
12. Ibid., pp. 232-8.
13. Irfan Habib, 'Usury in Medieval India', *Comparative Studies in Society and History*, vol. 6, no. 4 (July 1964), pp. 393-419.
14. For supplies to Surat. See Travenier, op. cit., p. 32.
15. Irfan Habib, 'Merchant Communities', *The Rise of Merchant Empires c. 1350-1750*, pp. 9-10.
16. *Amber Record* written by Sanghi Kalyan Das to Ramchand, dt. *Chait Vadi* 13, VS 1719/AD 1662.
17. *Amber Record* written by Gokal Das Ramji from *Pargana* Rewari, dt. *Fagun Sudi* 8, VS 1723/AD 1666.
18. *Amber Record* written by Vithaldas, Vijay Ram of *qasba* Kotla, dt. *Bhadwa Vadi* 8, VS 1722/AD 1665.
19. *Arzdasht* from Ramchandji to Ramsinghji, dt. *Chait Sudi* 8, VS 1740/AD 1683.
20. Ibid.
21. Mundy, *Travels of Peter Mundy*, p. 95.
22. Tavernier, *Travels in India*, pp. 32, 39.
23. *Selected Documents of Aurangzeb's Reign*, ed. Dr. Yusuf Hussain, Hyderabad, 1958, p. 18 (cf. Syed Aslam Ali, op. cit., p. 4).

24. Mundy, op. cit., pp. 96-8.
25. Salt was the most extensively supplied commodity. It was supplied upto Bengal by Banjaras. For further details see B.R. Grover, op. cit., pp. 235-9. Tavernier, op. cit., pp. 32-3; Francis Buchanan, op. cit., p. 203; Mundy, op. cit., p. 96; William Crooke, op. cit., p. 27.
26. *Factories, 1655-60,* pp. 75-6. A.I. Chicherov, *India Economic Development in the 16th-18th Century,* Moscow, 1971, p. 100.
27. Mundy, op. cit., p. 96.
28. *Amber Record* written by Kalyan Das, dt. *Chait Sudi* 6, VS 1722/AD 1665.
29. Syed Aslam Ali, op. cit., pp. 5-6.
30. *Amber Record* written by Tek Chand of *Pargana* Dausa, dt. *Chait Sudi* 4, VS 1743/AD 1686.
31. Nazir Akbarabadi, 'Banjara' for full poem see Appendix I.
32. John Malcolm, *Memories of Central India,* London, 1824, vol. II, pp. 152-3. Cf. Irfan Habib, 'Merchant Communities', op. cit., p. 11.
33. Russell and Lal, op. cit., p. 191.
34. *Arsattha, Pargana* Chatsu, dt. VS 1721/AD 1664.
35. Syed Aslam Ali, op. cit., pp. 8-9.
36. *Factories, 1618-21*, p. 102.
37. *Factories, 1634-6*, p. 187.
38. Syed Aslam Ali, op. cit., pp. 11-12.
39. *Factories, 1624-9*, p. 235; *Factories, 1645-50*, p. 297.
40. *Tuzuk-i-Jahangiri*, op. cit., vol. II, p. 233.
41. *Mirat,* vol. I, p. 303, cf. Syed Aslam Ali, op. cit., p. 17.
42. Ibid., p. 304, cf. S.A. Ali, op. cit., p. 17.
43. Tavernier, *Travels in India*, tr. V. Ball and (revised by) W. Crooke, vol. I, MacMillan, London, 1889, pp. 40-1.
44. Ranabir Chakravarti, *Trade and Traders in Early Indian Society*, Manohar, New Delhi, 2002, p. 193.

CHAPTER FOUR

Routes and En-route Conflicts of the Banjaras

THE BANJARAS TRAVELLED throughout the year except during the rainy season when roads became muddy and treacherous. Further, the Banjaras were travelling throughout the year with the *tandas*, without carrying the fodder so it was obvious for them to take the routes on which the grass and fodder for the animals was easily available. The routes used by Banjaras ran through fertile and directly administered regions which were well-traversed and safe from sudden violent disturbances and were chosen owing to the presence of grazing lands all along the routes.[1] Here before discussing the nature of conflicts between Banjaras and the local populace or state officials; I would like to discuss in brief about the prominent trade routes which were providing survival base to the wide nexus of the trade movement in the Indian subcontinent.

The geographical location of Rajasthan is so placed that it became a major land for the various in-land routes which facilated the travellers to connect north-western India with the central and west coast of India effectively. The prominent trade routes of Rajasthan during medieval centuries were following and even today these routes are in use for one or another mode of transport:

(i) Ajmer to Agra.[2]
(ii) Ajmer to Lahore.[3]
(iii) Ajmer to Ahmedabad.[4]
(iv) Ajmer to Malwa.[5]
(v) Jaipur to Karauli-Gwalior.[6]
(vi) Agra to Ahmedabad via Chittor;[7] and Chatsa Merta and Jalore.[8]
(vii) Delhi to Ahmedabad through Churu, Nagore, Jodhpur, Jalore and Sirohi.[9]
(viii) Agra and Delhi were connected with lower Sindh via Ajmer and Hindaun.[10]
(ix) Jodhpur to Peshawar.[11]
(x) Another route from Agra to Ajmer was via Hindaun, Lalsot and Mauzabad.[12]

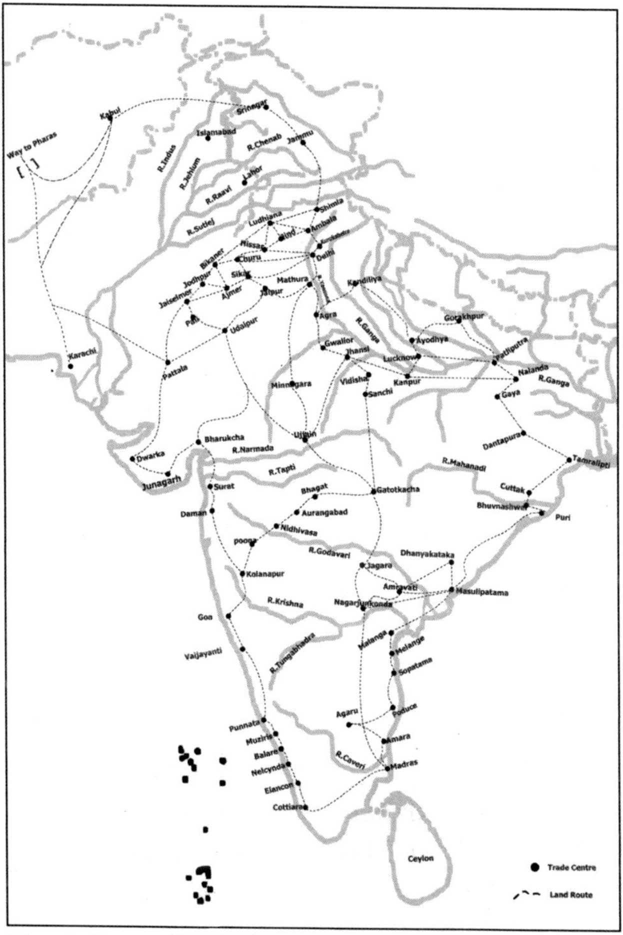

Map 1: Routes Travelled by Banjaras in Medieval Centuries (drawn by the author).

Map 2: Routes of the North-Western Region (drawn by the author).

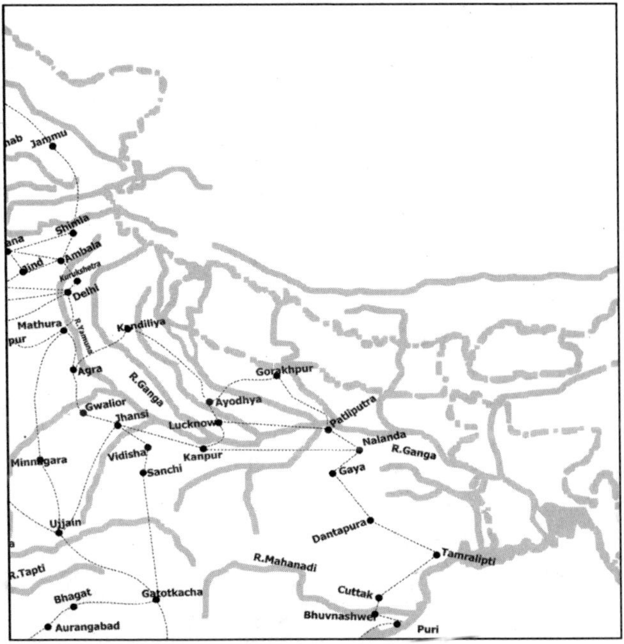

Map 3: Routes Undertaken by Banjaras in Eastern India (drawn by the author).

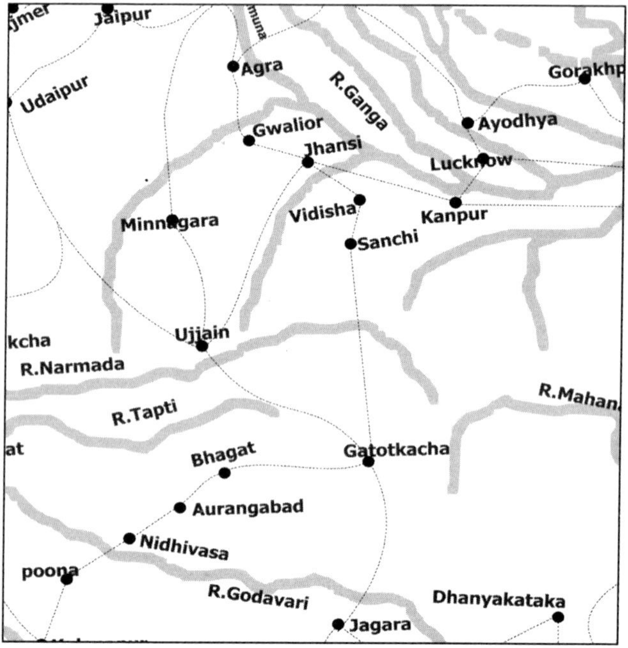

Map 4: *Carvan* Routes of Central India (drawn by the author).

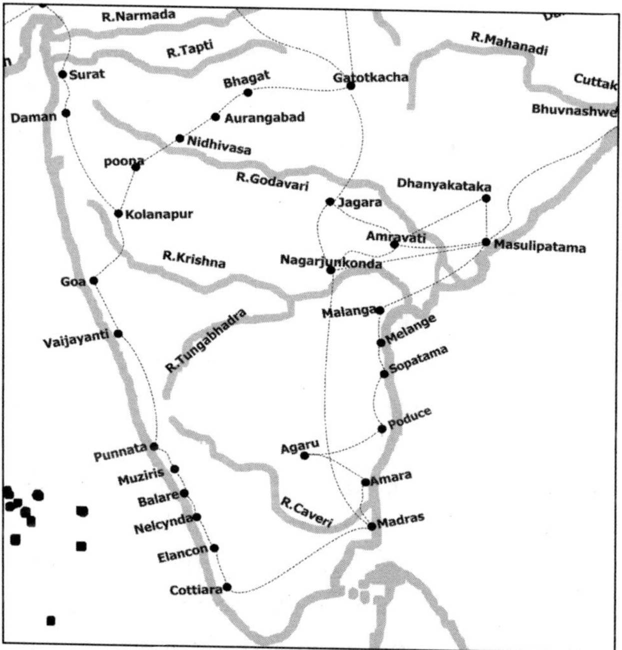

Map 5: Routes Marked by Banjaras in Peninsular India (drawn by the author).

(xi) Rajgarh to Khairpur through Churu and Bikaner[13]

(xii) Agra to Khairpur (Sindh) through Bikaner and Jaisalmer.[14]

(xiii) From Multan to Jaipur via Bahawalpur, Pugal, Bikaner, Churu, Sikar and Jodhpur.[15]

(xiv) Delhi to Khorasar through Nagpur, Jodhpur and Udaipur.

(xv) Agra to Ajmer via Delhi, Shahpura, Amber Narayana.[16]

The geographical location of Mewar between north-India and western-central India made it crucial for passage of trade and traffic.[17]

A 'route also ran from Anahilapura through Siddhapura, Candravati, Abu, Bhinmal, Nadol, Jalor, Bali, Pali, Ajmer and Naraina to Mathura.[18]

The purpose here of discussing the trade routes is to drive attention of the readers to an interesting fact that all these routes have a thick presence of the Banjara population travelling along with their *tandas*. Even today while travelling through these routes one can easily see the Banjara *carvans* with their cattle and members of *tanda*.

The Banjaras travelled throughout the year except during the rainy seasons to keep the supplies safe from rain water. The Banjaras were constantly travelling on these routes (see Map 1). Further, the pouring rain water was harmful for the goods like salt, sugar and food grains. Though the Banjaras maintained a large number of oxen, they never carried animal fodder with the *carvan* as it was impossible to carry fodder in such a large quantity. They fed their animals along the routes and nobody restricted them. The direct grazing of oxen from the soil while travelling reduced the cost of fodder and saved time and effort which went into stopping and feeding an animal. The grazing of animals directly from the fields was often the reason of conflict between the Banjaras and peasants. Usually the animal of the *carvan* were fed or grazed around the routes but while passing through the villages and *qasbas*, at times the animal were fed on the standing crops and due to it the Banjaras not only came in conflict with the peasants but also with the watchmen (*sahnas*) posted by the state to look after the standing crops under the system of *khet-batai* (division of standing crops). From an analysis of the nature of some disputes between the Banjaras and peasants and between the Banjaras and the *sahna* we can make some generalizations about the social tensions that affected the Banjaras.

While commenting on the movements of the

Banjaras, Francis Buchanan says that 'The people who transport salt and grain generally use asses or a very poor kind of bullock. These creatures get nothing to eat but what they can pick up by the side of the road.'[19] From the above description it is clear that Buchanan was not clear about the identity of the Banjaras who employed bullocks. The employment of asses was also very common during medieval times, because a donkey is capable of carrying nearly a load of 300-500 kg. Through double-loading the donkeys were able to carry nearly 450-500 kg. Occassionally the Banjaras used donkeys for transporting goods over short distances. Bullocks were their principle means of transport. Nowadays, the impoverished Banjaras only employ donkeys while they travel, and do rear cows, exclusively of *Nagauri* breed for commercial activities and in dry seasons they travel with the cowherds.

Peter Mundy's travel accounts provide a much deeper insight into the trading practices and the lifestyle of the Banjaras. According to him after unlading of their oxen, they turn them to a grazing ground which was nearby and nobody forbade them from doing so.[20] The observation of Mundy might have been about the forest and grazing grounds where the Banjaras' animals had free access due to favourable state policies. But we have come across a number of cases about the grazing of animals in the fields owned by the peasants. As noted earlier whenever the animals of Banjaras poached into the standing crops of the peasants, it became the cause of social tensions between the owner of the field and the concerned Banjaras. The state as mentioned before also appointed *sahnas* to protect and look after the standing crops under the *batai* system. The numerous recorded instances help us to understand the nature of conflict between the Banjaras and the *sahnas*. Similarly, whenever the Banjara's oxen were seen treading or eating standing crops, a fight between the peasants and Banjaras also ensued.

In AD 1632, Peter Mundy also made interesting observation about the grazing habits of a *tanda*. According to Mundy the Banjaras generally brought their oxen together and let them graze all over the plains by the river side.[21] His observation suggests that the Banjaras generally graze their animals outside the fields of the peasants. The grazing of animals in the pastures en-route without making any charges shows liberal attitude of state towards the Banjaras. The en-route nature of the grazing animals was also described by Lt. Col. Fitzclarence. He says that 'I have seen them with droves of 50,000 bullocks. They do not move about two miles an hour, as the cattle are allowed to graze as they proceed on the march.'[22] This testimony has been uncritically accepted by William Irvin. However, our evidence suggests that the major cause of the en-route conflicts between the Banjaras and peasants was the grazing of animals directly from the fields, thereby causing harm to standing crops.

There is plentiful evidence recorded in the *Arsatthas* especially of those *parganas* which are situated on the trade routes of the Banjara *carvan*. In this regard some interesting information is available in the *hasil firohi* column of the *Arsatthas* (see Appendix II). The evidences cover a period between *c.* 1665 and 1750 CE. The information pertains to *parganas* of Tonk, Dausa, Lalsot, Malpura, Fagui, Bhartari, Chatsu, Ao, Narayana and Pachewar. With a close perusal of nearly fifty-four cases, some interesting patterns about the nature of en-route conflicts involving the Banjaras and peasants or state officials, etc., becomes discernible. Before we discuss the actual nature of individual cases, it is necessary to mention the parties involved in these cases.

The Banjaras invariably came in conflict with the peasants of villages or *qasbas* which were located on the trade routes. Destruction of standing crops by the oxen of Banjaras was the main cause of tension between the villagers and the Banjaras. Out of a total of fifty-four cases given at the end of this work, nearly thirty-eight cases clearly indicate the destruction of the crops of peasants by the bullocks of the Banjaras. The Banjaras were penalized by the state for causing harm to the standing crops. Our sources are silent whether the peasants were compensated for the loss or not. In *pargana* Tonk high penalties were imposed on the Banjaras on account of crop spoliation. For instance, Kesara Banjara was fined Rs. 35 for destroying standing crops.[23] In another case a Banjara was subjected to a penalty of Rs. 47 for destroying the crop of Chaudhari Pemaram and Tara Chand.[24] Similarly, Haider Mani *Nayak* and Chitar Banjara were subjected to a penalty of Rs. 23 and 21 for causing harm to the standing crops in *pargana* Lalsot and Malpura respectively.[25] Whenever, an ordinary Banjara's ox destroyed the standing crops, the amount of penalty was abysmally low. Normally, such Banjaras had to pay a penalty ranging between Re. 1 and Rs. 5. It appears that nominal penalties were fixed on those

Banjaras whose bullocks caused destruction to low value crops. Whenever, any Banjara's bullock caused destruction to cash crops, a relatively high penalty was imposed. For example when the bullocks of Kesara Banjara caused destruction to the *var* (mustard) crop, he was subjected to a penalty of Rs. 14.[26] In another case Girdha Banjara had to pay a fine of Rs. 11 for causing destruction of *paagu* (oil seed) crop in a village of *pargana* Bhartari.[27] The *Nayaks* who were the head of a *tanda* were usually subjected to higher penalties. Clearly, the state took into consideration the gravity of an offence and the value of loss while deciding the amount of penalties.

In the region of our study, *khet-batai* was a dominant form of revenue assessment and collection. Under this system standing crops were divided between the cultivator and the state. The state usually posted *sahnas* to the villages for looking after the fields. Whenever, the bullocks of any Banjara strayed into that portion of the field which belonged to the state, the *sahna* immediately came in conflict with the Banjara. Usually, such conflicts degenerated into open warfare between the *sahna* and the Banjaras. Interestingly, in all the conflicts involving the *sahna* and Banjaras, the penalty was comparatively nominal, ranging between Re. 1 and Rs. 5 only. Such a liberal stance of the state towards the defaulting Banjaras is quite intriguing. Perhaps the officials let off the Banjaras lightly as the latter played a crucial role in the process of marketing the grains owned by the state. If the protection of crops was necessary, the state also had to find ways and means to market the surplus collected from the peasants. As the Banjaras played a central role in transporting grains, etc., minor irritations caused in the course of their movement had to be ignored.

The Banjaras also came in open conflict with the *vachhait* (purchaser/broker) who came from outside in the *qasba* markets. The *vachhait* might have posed some competition to Banjaras regarding purchase of some goods. A lot of haggling was involved in the process of weighing of goods before loading or at the time of unloading. Many a times it was found that the weight of goods was less than expected. For example, in *qasba* Fagui a conflict between the *vachhaits* and Banjaras occurred when some goods (out of total) were found missing. A penalty of Rs. 10 was charged from the Banjaras.[28] In yet another case of a fight between the *vachhait* and the Banjaras in *qasba* Tonk, the latter were subjected to a high penalty of Rs. 41.[29] Apparently, the state was keen to desist the Banjaras from any unruly acts which could cause dislocation in the smooth working of *qasba* markets. In other words, the state from time to time had to discipline the Banjaras and others in a market place. Sometimes the Banjaras were penalized for causing loss of some goods assigned to them. For example, Gidhwa Bohra of Tonk had given some pots of *khand* (sugar) to the Banjaras. While receiving the pots at *qasba* Fagui, the Bohra found two of his pots of *khand* missing. The *faujdar* imposed a fine of Rs. 10 on the offending Banjara.[30] In two other similar cases the Banjaras were accused of missing some rice. Both the incidents occurred in *qasba* Dausa. Penalties ranging from Rs. 4 to 10 were imposed.[31] Perhaps the variation in the amount of penalties depended on the value of the lost goods.

Since destruction of crops entailed loss of revenues, the state had to fine the offending Banjaras for doing harm to the crops. Peasants had to be protected as they were the primary producers of grain. The Banjara had to be protected because without their help grain could not be converted into cash. The magnitude of penalties on the Banjaras was determined by the extent of harm and the nature of the crop. From the aforementioned cases, it appears that these penalties were quite moderate. But whenever the Banjaras tried to create disturbances in the market place, they were fined heavily even if the matter was trivial. Our evidence shows that most of the conflicts involving the Banjaras and the peasants were resolved locally either by the *faujdar* or an *amil*. We have not come across any armed conflicts between the Banjaras and the state armies. Apart from conflicts between the Banjaras on the one hand and peasants, officials and *vachhaits* on the other, conflicts between two *tandas* are also mentioned.

Tavernier, while travelling in Mughal India in *c.* 1669 makes an observation about the efforts made by the Mughal emperor on the eruption of hostilities between the *tandas*. The Mughals tried to keep the *carvan* members happy and pacified. From time to time the rulers checked the movement of Banjara *carvans*. The Mughal emperor not only ensured that the *tandas* of Banjaras should remain peaceful but also made efforts to kept them happy and satisfied by presenting gifts and robes of honour (*sir-o-pao*) to the *tanda* leaders.[32]

As the fight between the two *tandas* was a serious matter, local officials were always on alert whenever the *tandas* entered their jurisdiction. The Banjaras seldom liked the intervention of local authorities in their internal matters. They preferred direct audience with the ruler. Sometimes the local *bhomia* also tried to divert the course of the Banjara movement. For example, when Tulsidass Hamirdeka, a *bhomia*, tried to stop a Banjara *carvan* from reaching its fixed destination, the Banjara threatened to take up the matter with the *darbar*.[33]

The Banjaras lived a life of rivalry and brotherhood. However, on numerous occasions fights erupted between two *tandas*. The underlying causes for these fights could be many but largely the *tandas* fought among themselves on account of mainly three reasons. As the *tanda* moved through narrow pathways, two *tandas* could fight for first clearance. Tapan Raychaudhuri suggests that the reason for fierce fighting amongst *tandas* could be the right to passage.[34] Intermixing of oxen of two *tandas* at the time of halting in night could be another reason of inter *tanda* conflicts. The fear of potential loss in the next market could also push two *tandas* into a situation of conflict. Each *tanda* tried to keep itself in the forefront of the general movement of the *carvans* in order to fetch better prices of their goods. The other reason for such fights amongst *tandas* might have been the late arrival in the markets. If a *tanda* delayed the delivery of goods it had to make compensation for the resultant loss.

C.A. Bayly while making his observation about the nature of conflicts between the Banjaras and peasants says that such conflicts took place in the summer season only.[35] He says that during the months of summer, fodder becomes scanty; therefore the Banjaras turned to stray their animals into the peasants fields. But our sources clearly indicate that the conflicts between the Banjara nomads and the settled people were perennial. For example, in *mauza* Rewari Malik Rehmat Khan and Budan Khan fought with the Banjaras who were destroying the fields in the month of *Asoj* (September- October).[36] There are many cases which would qualify the firm position taken by Bayly regarding the timing of enroute conflicts.

At the end it could be said that the Banjaras being a community of armed transporters engaged in long distance trade and inevitably came in conflict with the villagers due to their animals' reliance on grazing in the fields. The medieval state being conscious of optimizing its revenues had to protect standing crops from any harm by the oxen of the Banjaras. Similarly, the state's reliance on the Banjaras to market its grain in distant places made them indulgent towards the Banjaras. Keeping these imperatives in mind, the state intervened in any conflict between the Banjaras and others. Nevertheless, despite occasional tensions between the Banjaras and other social groups, the Banjaras were much sought after because of their indispensable role as traders and transporters; in the economy of medieval India.

NOTES

1. Shireen Moosvi, *People, Taxation and Trade in Mughal India*, Oxford University Press, New Delhi, 2008, p. 291.
2. Abul Fazal, *Akbarnama,* vol. II, p. 511. This route from Agra to Ajmer passed through Mandhakar, Fatehpur, Khanwa, Kasroha, Basawar, Toda, Kalawali, Kharandi, Disu, Phul Mahal, Sanganir, Jhak, Sahhun, Kajbil.
3. Richard Burn, *The Cambridge History of India,* vol. III, Cambridge University Press, 1934, p. 119. The en-route towns from Ajmer to Lahore were Merta, Narnaul, Shadiwal and Lahore.
4. Nizamuddin Ahmad, *Tabaqat-i-Akbari*, vol. II, pp. 410-12. The places en-route were Pali, Jalaur, Pattanwal, Disa, Balisana, Pattan.
5. Beni Prasad, *History of Jahangir*, Indian Press, Allahabad, 1940, pp. 235-6. The route from Ajmer to Malwa passed through Deorai, Ransir, Ujjain and Mandu.

6. B.L. Gupta, *Trade and Commerce in Rajasthan during the 18th Century,* Jaipur Publishing House, Jaipur, 1987, p. 135.
7. H.C. Verma, *Medieval Routes to India: Baghdad to Delhi: A Study of Trade and Military Routes,* Naya Prakash, Calcutta, 1978, p. 113.
8. J. De Laet, *The Empire of the Great Mughals,* tr. John J.S. Hoyland, The British India Press, Bombay, 1928, pp. 64-6.
9. P.W. Powlett, *Gazetter of the Bikaner State,* Authority Government of India, Calcutta, 1868, p. 251.
10. H.C. Verma, *Medieval Routes to India,* p. 113.
11. Ibid.
12. De Laet, *The Empire of the Great Mughals,* tr. John S. Hoyland, The British India Press, Bombay, 1928, pp. 64-6.
13. James Tod, *Annals and Antiquities,* vol. II, Smith, Elder Co., rpt., Routledge Kegan Paul, London, 1957, pp. 523-5.
14. Ibid., pp. 603-8.
15. G.N. Sharma, *Social Life in Medieval Rajasthan (1500-1800): With Special Reference to the Impact of Mughal Influence,* Lakshmi Narain Agarwal, Agra, 1968, pp. 323-5.
16. A close study of these routes helps us to understand that some of major trading centres and market centres of medieval India are on these routes. The major centres such as Agra, Delhi, Amber, Ajmer, Bikaner, Churu, Jodhpur, Chittor, Sambhari, etc., are connected by these routes. Presently the rail routes of Indian railways are effectively connecting all these centres.
17. Nandini Sinha Kapur, *State Formation in Rajasthan: Mewar During the Seventh-Fifteenth Centuries,* Manohar, New Delhi, 2002, p. 64.
18. Ibid., pp. 64-5.
19. Francis Buchanan, *A Journey from Madras Through the*

Countries of Mysore, Canara and Malabar, vol. I, pp. 179 and 206.

20. Peter Mundy, *Travels of Peter Mundy*, p. 96; Russell, op. cit., p. 169.
21. Ibid., p. 98.
22. Irvin, *The Army of the Indian Mughals*, p. 192.
23. *Arsattha, Pargana* Tonk, VS 1768/AD 1711.
24. Ibid.
25. *Arsattha, Pargana* Lalsot, VS 1794/AD 1737, *Arsattha, Pargana* Malpura, VS 1799/AD 1742.
26. *Arsattha, Pargana* Narayana, VS 1781/AD 1724.
27. *Arsattha, Pargana* Bhartari, VS 1722/AD 1665.
28. *Arsattha, Pargana* Fagui, VS 1778/AD 1721.
29. *Arsattha, Pargana* Tonk, VS 1768/AD 1711.
30. *Arsattha, Pargana* Fagui, VS 1778/AD 1721.
31. *Arsattha, Pargana* Fagui, VS 1790/AD 1733, VS 1778/AD 1721.
32. Tavernier, op. cit., pp. 39-45.
33. *Arzdasht, Pargana* Amber, dt. *Kati Vadi,* VS 1751/AD 1694.
34. Raychaudhuri, op. cit., p. 354.
35. Bayly, *Rulers, Townsmen and Bazars,* p. 222.
36. *Arzdasht, Mauza* Rewari, dt. *Aasoj Sudi* 13, VS 1751/AD 1694.

CHAPTER FIVE

Process of Criminalization and Twilight of the Banjaras

TRANSPORT WAS CONSIDERED as a key factor in expansion and growth of medieval economy. The inland transport activities were essentially based on employment of an animal for transportation and it was key to feed the costal maritime trade.[1]

The Banjaras enjoyed a great status as the transporters of the empire and attempts were made by state to accommodate them at all times so that the economic activities of the state shall never suffer. The Banjara community has served in close coordination with the state since the time of Alauddin Khilji. The agents of British Empire also hired the services of these transporters. Being the transporters of empires the Banjaras served the sultanate, Mughal state and British Empire equally. The method of transportation was primitive in nature in which the draught animal ox was employed to carry the goods. The members of *carvan* walked besides the laden animal. The technique used for comfortable, effective and balanced loading on the animal was the 'double-loading' technique. In which two equal weighing bales were hung on each side of the ox. This technique was effective and comfortable because it allowed the animal to walk swiftly as the load is balanced on both the sides. Secondly, the owner of the cattle was relived of the burden of checking the bales again and again while the animal is on move as both the bundles of each side were tied together near the hump (see Plate 12). Later in nineteenth century the Banjaras also started employing donkeys. The interesting fact to note here is that the Banjaras being the efficient transporters of the times never tried to employ the most effective and fastest draught animal namely horse. The horse was the most popular animal during medieval times because of its speed, intelligence and also effectivness in the warfields. The possible reasons for not engaging the horses in the transportation activity were, the difficulties and challenges to be faced, for keeping the horses healthy and fit. An insightful reading of the interesting work indicates that it was significantly difficult to keep a horse in healthy condition.[2] It could have been a major factor for discouraging the employment of horses in the transportation activity, as the kind of animal needed was the one which required minimum care and maintenance. Secondly, the horse was a representative of the elite class because of its usage as a war-animal. The cavalry was also the main component of the vast Mughal army. Due to nature of its utility in Mughal army the horse was a highly priced commodity and its high demand for fulfilling the requirements of war-training and war, made it a rather expensive proposition. The demand for horses in medieval cavalry was significantly high and ever continuing.

The animals which are listed as draught animals due to the nature and style of engagement concocted for these animals in load carrying activities are donkey, camel, horse, mule and ox. Amongst these enlisted animals the ox is the most suitable animal for long distance transportation activities due to its consistent speed, nature of grazing (picking from fields while walking), non-requirement of special food supplements, minimum requirement of water and ability to adapt (quickly) in the changing terrain.

Due to these qualities of ox the *carvan* never required to carry the fodder of any specific quality or any other thing for the animal, which if required would have added load to the en-route consumable items. The animal is also a comfortable acclimatizer and it further eased the challenges to be encountered en-route. All these specifications of the animal and absence of specific maintenance and care; made ox an obvious choice of the Banjaras for its employment in long-distance trading.

Here, I am escaping from the discussion on the extent of ox employment by Banjaras as it has been discussed in great detail in the earlier chapters. An overall study of the Banjara customs, their role in economy and their life style helps us to understand that the Banjaras were engaged in transportation, trading and pastoral activities. Large varieties of goods were transported by them throughout India.[3] Large volume of internal trade was carried out in food grains, various agricultural produces and non-agricultural products such as salt.[4] A prominent role was played by Banjaras in transportation and trading activities of south India.[5] Transport was the key factor for the expansion and development of the medieval economy. The effective transportation system helped in collecting the agricultural items produced in the country-side and made them available in the town markets. The inter-regional and local exchange of commodities and goods and vast production of diverse agricultural produce made transporter an essential ingredient of the economy. The Banjaras were the transporters of empire and acted as the factors of *banias.*[6] The Banjara community is a heterogeneous group with dominant resemblance to the Rajasthani culture such as the language spoken is Marwari and Banjari[7] (a dialect very close to Marwari), clothes (*ghaghras, odhni, chund / shing*; a cone shaped silver ornament worn over head by married women, *angi, dhoti, pagri, cholana*, etc.).[8] The Banjaras travelled and transported the non-perishable goods to nearly all parts of India and especially to the arid zones or the areas which were not well connected with the riverine network. Braving the hazards of the inhospitable and difficult terrains the Banjaras kept the transport alive in remote areas which had no facility or were supplied with minimum facilities. Delhi and Agra were the main administrative centres during medieval period and the state exercised its control over north India from these centres. These centres were halting destinations for the multidirectional travellers. Similarly, these centres were crucial for the travelling Banjaras. As the Banjaras were acting on behalf of the state, therefore, their coordination with these centres was essential. Banjaras also served as the commissariats of the empires. They 'served in the transport department of the Mughal armies and with the British troops in the last century'.[9]

Being the suppliers of the army the Banjaras played some remarkable roles. In AD 1630 Banjaras reached Deccan as part of Shah Jahan's invading forces.[10] The role of Banjaras as the commissariat of Mughal army is evident from the saying of a Mughal commander, who said to the Banjara leaders 'I do not mind if you burn my crop and poison my wells, so long as you feed my armies'.[11] The Banjaras were considered useful and were also employed by the British armies. The Banjaras helped the John Company to win the war of Seringapatam.[12] He further notes 'it was to the timely supply of provisions brought by the Banjaras that the safety of the British army may be ascribed'.[13]

The role of Banjaras in the supply line for the armies is clearly evident from these instances and reports made by the British officials themselves. 'In the late eighteenth century they were described as a people of "useful class" without whom the army was helpless'.[14] On various other occasions the Banjaras were hired by the Company which is a clear indication to the fact that the transportation of goods was impossible in the hinterlands of India without the help of Banjaras. The Banjaras swiftly survived the change of empire from Mughal to the British. But what happened in the first half of the nineteenth century which pushed British Empire to label them as a 'Criminal' group? By the 1840s, the Banjaras were seen as a criminal group.[15] Was it the inability of the British governance to distinguish between the groups who were given to the criminal activities (such as the *thugees*) or was it the common feature of 'wandering' amongst the groups (Banjaras, Nat, Bhils, Lohars, etc.) of medieval times that made the British Empire to collect all of these communities under one single umbrella?

Here being the student of history I want to pause and think – why such an important heterogeneous community; who was known for its honesty, safety and protection to trade while travelling and was an effective facilitators of transportation had been enlisted as a criminal community. Second, the Banjaras were not at all hostile to the British and were even helping supply lines of the Company. Third, the

Banjaras were efficient transporters who moved in *tandas* and could have been easily inducted into the British system. Besides all these positive indicators, the Company didn't make efforts to distinguish the Banjaras from the regular wandering groups, why? In order to understand the component of criminal activity and to label any act of communities as criminal let us first focus on the big question, what was a crime and who was a criminal? The crime as defined in legal dictionary is an act committed or omitted, in violation of a public law, either forbidding or commanding it; a breach or violation of some public right or duty, due to a whole community. After much effort I can say that it is a performance of an action/act or omission of a particular action/act to which a citizen of a country is bound, and it is punishable by law of land. The irony here is that the Banjaras were not doing any act/activity which was prohibited by law. Here and there various instances appear in our records which indicate to rowdiness and unconstitutional behaviour of the Banjaras such as, feeding the animals (bullocks) in the standing fields; quarrel amongst Banjara *tandas*; fight with state officials; etc.[16] Cattle lifting was the most common offence committed by Banjaras throughout India.[17]

Writing about Banjaras of north India, Robert Vardy notes:

Banjaras have been on Indian scene for more than seven hundred years. While others have crumbled, these nomadic communities have demonstrated their versatility by surviving several onslaughts against their way of life in the nineteenth century, Banjara *tandas* confronted with extinction, evolved modes of adaptation which featured permanent settling, criminality, and development of the draft oxen trade.[18]

Amongst the various sub-divisions of Banjaras, the Mathurias group (named after Mathura) was not accommodated under the criminal group and were economically better off.[19] The tag of criminal was limited only to the moving herds!

Highway robbery, cattle lifting, sheep stealing, kidnapping, ransacking grain-pits, dacoity, pilfering from carts (both moving and halting), smuggling of opium, blackmailing for restoration of stolen cattle are most common form of the crimes committed by the Banjaras.[20] Generally, the observance of the above mentioned unconstitutional behaviour were settled by punitive measures but the performance of these offences never allowed the Banjaras to be branded 'criminal' forever in the medieval centuries. During the nineteenth century the wandering nature of the groups was the main component to label the groups as criminals. 'Wandering mendicants and mobile vagrant groups were most liable to be classed as criminals'.[21] While travelling in the region of Awadh William Sleeman notes that besides the Gosains and Bairagis 'the other bands wander about as Benjaras, Khunjurs, Nats'.[22]

All the notorious, violent and criminal activities of the Banjaras in and around the Gorakhpur *sarkar* came to an end with the relinquishment of this territory to the East India Company.[23] C.A. Bayly suggests that the role of Banjaras in the British territories was restricted due to the three developments. First, they were subordinate to the merchants and the newly constituted military commissariat department. Second, the dwindling pasture lands and last, series of cattle endemics in 1820s and 1830s added to their woes.[24]

I hereby agree with the scholar that 'conceptualizing crime on a pan-Indian scale from the 1820s onward was thus heavily influenced by the idea of mobility'.[25] The inability of the Company officials to control the movement of this particular wandering group (Banjaras) and to bring it under surveillance was a significant reason to label them as criminal. As it is mentioned that, 'mobility was rather an integral part of the discourse through which colonial state understood criminality in India'.[26] An interesting and fascinating piece of information based in eighteenth century highlights the efforts made by the Banjaras, to give up its nomadic-wandering character and it depicts the interest of the Banjaras to carve a territory of their own and settle down. In the eastern part of the Awadh kingdom the Banjaras conducted various violent acts against the hereditary chiefs as they were sturdy enough due to the numerical strength of the *tanda*. The emergence of Banjaras on the political horizons of *sarkar* Gorakhpur was dominant enough as no individual hereditary chieftain was able to grapple with the menace and lawlessness of the Banjaras. To check the threat of Banjara onslaught, the Bisin Raja of Majhauli had deserted a large portion of his estate to the newly established estate of Tamkhanli and Padrauna. This was to create a neutral territory or buffer zone between his estate (Majhauli) and the Banjara domain on the eastern side.[27] The efforts of Banjaras helped them to establish their own *ta'alluqa*. It is confirmed from a letter collected in *Mansur-ul-Maktubat*, which was written by Santokh Rai, *Munshi* of Safdar Jung. The letter was addressed to Mauhmmad Shah and Wazir Qamruddin Khan in order to report the whereabouts of Nawab Badr-ul-din Khan; who became a wandering ascetic and his exact location was unchartered. They heard last about him when he went to 'Pargana Hansi and Gorakhpur in the *Ta'alluqa* of the Banjaras'.[28] Interestingly, various European travelogues and reports provide ample illustrations where the Banjaras have been praised for their effective mobility and consignments.[29] Generally, the Banjaras were employed by the Company for efficient transportation and without them the army was helpless. The vibrancy of the Indian trade was due to the Banjaras and similarly, the success of the armies and its campaign also relied on the supplies ensured by the Banjaras.

With the coming of the British Company rule, the socio-cultural milieu of India underwent a change, due to the rampant commercial desire of the Company for evermore profits. The Banjaras became the necessary victims of the most ambitious economic project of the Company, the Railways. The idea of wooden-railed wagon originated in Germany in the sixteenth century and the first steam locomotive was used in Britain. In AD 1793, the first cast iron rail road was constructed, which was a mile-long. Consequently, in AD 1820, John Birkenshaw introduced a method of rolling wrought iron rails, which were used from then onwards. Successfully, the railways attained potential rapidity in the movement of traffic due to which more and more lines were built. A lecture titled 'Lecture on Rail Roads,' was delivered by William Jackson on 12 January 1829 before Massachusetts: a charitable mechanic association at Boston, emphasizing on the great discovery of the century (Railways) which will connect the remotest corners, will speed up the trade activities and enhance profits.[30] Jackson himself was member of the association.[31] Further, in his speech before the association (of Massachusetts) Jackson highlights the great contributions which have been made by the merchants, sailors and mechanics of Massachusetts association to the civilized and uncivilized world.[32] The countries who have received and benefited from the mechanical inventions of the Massachusetts association were West Indies, South America, Europe and India.[33] The prominence of trade activities in these countries greatly needed rapidity as per his idea and the introduction of railways was the answer to it. This is also true in the sense that during contemporary times no other mode of speedy transportation was visible. The vacuum of the same provided space for the widespread construction of railways; as a efficient, effective and speedy mode for transportation. The 1840s were the biggest decade for the railway growth in Britain. In the 1840s, when the decade began, railway lines in Britain were few and scattered but, within ten years, a complete network system had been laid down and the vast majority of towns and villages had rail connection. Simultaneously, the pressure for building the railways in India came from London and thereafter nearly for a century the basic policies and management of the railways was controlled from London. Correspondingly, in India the criminalization of the transporting community of the Banjaras has started.[34] The plan of building railways in India was guided by the hope of connecting the economic, military and political fronts. The railway was able to tie the different parts of India more closely and together, with a regulated to and fro movement of the traffic. This was a miracle for the Indian masses, who were not at all aware of such a fast mode of transportation. On the other hand for the trading communities it was an invocation for adding speed to the trade. Apparently, that was the reason for the traders of

India to participate in the railway building activity. The first proposals for construction of railways in India were presented in 1844 to East India Company in London by (1) East Indian Railway Company (EIR) headed by R. Mc Donald Stephenson and (2) Great Indian Peninsula Railway Company (GIPR). George Stephenson, the inventor of Locomotive was one of the first Directors of GIPR and his son Robert Stephenson was appointed as the consulting engineer based at London. Both East Indian Railways (EIR) and Great Indian Peninsula Railways (GIPR) were incorporated in England for the purpose of constructing railway lines in Calcutta and Bombay presidencies respectively. Though, GIPR Company was formed in 1844, George Stephenson could not see his locomotives run on Indian soil as he died in AD 1848.

Lord Hardinge (*r.* 23 July 1844 to 12 January 1848), was the Governor-General of India at this point of time. He considered the proposals from political, military and commercial point of view and thought that the Court of Directors of East India Company should liberally give assistance to private capitalists who are willing to make railways in India without waiting for proof that the construction of railways in India should yield reasonable profit. The Court of Directors suggested that the first attempt in this direction shall be made on a limited scale due to some difficulties foreseen.

The native traders and merchants played a crucial role in building of the railway in India. The most prominent role was played by the Bengali merchant prince Dwarkanath Tagore. In AD 1844, Dwarkanath's firm called Carr, Tagore & Company, was reported to have offered to raise one-third of the capital required for building a railway from Calcutta north-west to the coal fields above Burdwan.[35] The introduction of railways in Indian landscape gave a severe blow to the Banjara transporters. The transportation mode of Banjaras (pack-oxen) was replaced with the far more effective railway system. The eclipse of Banjaras due to the Railways was noticed by a few British officials. Ibbetson notes 'the railway is fast destroying the carrying trade of these people except in the mountain tracts'.[36] Similarly, William Crooke records 'large gangs of Banjara merchants in the old days conveyed the products of central India and received in return iron and brass ware, cloth and salt. The region has now been tapped by direct railway communication with Calcutta and Bombay'.[37]

Overall, it could be said that the activities such as building of railways in England, the proposal to introduce and build railways in India and labeling of the Banjaras as a criminal community and their elimination from the economic panorama of Indian continent were connected activities controlled by the British. It is quite a possibility that the community was labelled under the criminal category because the Company was very well aware that after the introduction of the railways in Indian subcontinent, the Company will no more need these wandering native transporters who were difficult to identify and couldn't be taken under surveillance and were hard to be fixed in one particular space. Second, the introduction of railways will added up to the profits and will speed up the transportation of goods from one place to another, under guards and, the diverse weather conditions of the continent would no more hamper and delay the trade which was always a limitation with the laden-animal transportation system. Third, the railways would expand the internal as well as the external trade and the Company would have complete and direct control. The chances of margin cutting and hiding profits would also be eliminated. Fourth, the railways would remove the dependence of Company on the native transporters (Banjaras) to reach the far and remotest corners of the country to collect the raw material. The efficiency of the railways can be accessed from the comment made by W.H. Moreland on the transport of foodstuff by the Banjaras. He says that 'an entire season's traffic would be equivalent to an amount which a railway could carry over an equal distance in less than a week'.[38] Ironically, the so called 'criminal' community of Banjaras was employed as the labour in various rail building activities by the Company.[39] To bring the discussion to a halt it could be said that the concurrent events (exhaustive railway networking in England, proposal to build railways in India and enlisting of the criminal tribes and communities and lastly the employment of Banjaras in construction of rail routes and laying of tracks) in 1840s are an indicator for the scholars to locate the source material and establish a link between the events, to trace back the aim and reason behind the occurence of the events. Was the introduction of railway an effort to boost the economy or was it an intelligently devised mechanism to eliminate the natives from their hereditary professions? or was it an exercise by Company to gain full control over the economy? The various questions are still unanswered due to the lack of source material but certainly a link could be established.

NOTES

1. Ashin Das Gupta, *The World of the Indian Ocean Merchant c. 1500-1800: Collected Essays of Ashin Das Gupta*; compiled by Uma Das Gupta, with an introduction by Sanjay Subrahmanyam, Oxford University Press, Delhi, 2004.
2. R.B.A. Choudhary, 'The Horse and the Mughal Military Culture in Transition, 1526-1795', an unpublished M. Phil. dissertation submitted to the Department of History, University of Delhi, 2014, pp. 135-95.
3. M. Kennedy, *The Criminal Classes in India,* Mittal Publication, Delhi, 1985, p. 5.
4. Tapan Raychaudhuri and Irfan Habib (eds.), *The Cambridge Economic History of India*, p. 331; Tod, *Annals and Antiquities,* vol. II, pp. 126-33.
5. Joseph J. Brennig, 'Textile Producers and Production in Late Seventeenth Century Coromandel', *The Indian Economic Social History Review (IESHR),* December 1986, vol. 23, no. 4, pp. 333-55.
6. Masanori Sato and B.L. Bhadani, *The Economy and Polity of Rajasthan: Study of Kota and Marwar (17th-19th Centuries),* Publication Scheme, Jaipur, 1997, p. 104.
7. Bhagirathi Chowdhury, 'Banjara', in Sachchidananda and R.R. Parsad (eds.), *Encyclopaedic Profile of Indian Tribes,* Discovery Publishing House, New Delhi, 1996, p. 66.
8. Kennedy, *The Criminal Classes in India,* op. cit., p. 4.
9. Ibid., p. 5.

10. Russell, op. cit., p. 168; Brennig, 'Textile Producers and Production in Late Seventeenth Century Coromandel', op. cit., p. 336.
11. Bayly, *Rulers, Townsmen and Bazaars*, p. 29.
12. Captian Briggs, 'Account of the Origin, History and Manners of the Race of Men Called Bunjaras', *Transactions of the Literary Society of Bombay*, vol. I, London, 1819, p. 183.
13. Ibid.
14. Nitin Sinha, 'Mobility, Control and Criminality in Early Colonial India, 1760s-1850s', *IESHR*, vol. 45, January 2008, p. 8.
15. Ibid., p. 8.
16. See Appendix II
17. Kennedy, *The Criminal Classes in India,* pp. 2-6.
18. Robert Varady, 'North Indian Banjaras: Their Evolution as Transporters', *South Asia: Journals of South Asian Studies,* vol. 2, issues 1-2, 1979, pp. 11-18.
19. Kennedy, *The Criminal Classes in India,* p. 4.
20. Ibid., pp. 4-9.
21. Nitin Sinha, *Communication and Colonialism in Eastern India: Bihar, 1760s-1880s*, Anthem Press, London & New York, 2012, p. 122.
22. William Sleeman, *The History of Thugs and Phansigars of India*, Carey & Hart, Philadelphia, 1839, p. 46.
23. H.R. Nevill, *Distirct Gazatteers,* vols. 44-5. Cf. S.Z.H. Jafri, *Awadh from Mughal to Colonial Rule: Studies in the Anatomy of a Transformation,* Gyan Publishing House, Delhi, 2016 (rpt.), p. 124. Here after *Awadh from Mughal to Colonial Rule.*
24. Bayly, *Rulers, Townsmen and Bazaars*, p. 221.

25. Sinha, 'Mobility, Control and Criminality in Early Colonial India', p. 14.
26. Jafri, *Awadh from Mughal to Colonial Rule*, pp. 194-5. See fn. 17.
27. Ibid.
28. Awadhi Lal, *Insha-i-Mansur* or *Mansur-ul-Muktubat.* The only known copy of this manuscript is preserved at Tagore Library at Lucknow University. Cf. Jafri, *Awadh from Mughal to Colonial Rule*, pp. 121 and 124.
29. See chapter 'The Banjaras as Transporters'.
30. William Jackson, 'A Lecture on Rail Roads, Delivered on January 12, 1829: Before the Massachusetts: A Charitable Mechanic Association', printed by Crocker & Brewster, Washington Street, Boston, 1829.
31. Ibid., p. 1.
32. Ibid., p. 20.
33. Ibid.
34. Sinha, 'Mobility, Control and Criminality in Early Colonial India', *IESHR,* vol. 45, January 2008, p. 8.
35. Indian Railways History, http://www.irfca.org/
36. Ibbetson, *Punjab Castes*, op. cit., p. 254.
37. William Crooke, *The North-Western Provinces of India: Their History, Ethnology and Administration*, Methuen & Co., London, 1897, p. 27.
38. Raychaudhuri and Habib, *The Cambridge Economic History of India*, op. cit., p. 339.
39. Rana P. Behal and Marcel van der Linden (eds.), *Coolies, Capital and Colonialism: Studies in Indian Labour History*, Cambridge University Press, Cambridge, 2007, pp. 90-112.

CHAPTER SIX

Conclusion

AS HAS BEEN discussed in the preceding chapters, various classes of merchants were engaged in inland commercial operations. The trade activities included complex functioning and variety of classes and communities were organizing the different layers of it, at different levels. They differed not only in the scale of their commercial activity but also at certain measures of specialization. In the chain of exchanges linking the producers to the ultimate consumer in the local or distant markets, different groups performed distinct functions. The peace provided by the Mughals throughout the subcontinent, patronage extended to diverse and wide variety of craft industries and maintenance of a vast salaried class, comprising soldiers and retainers led to the growth of a well organized and consolidated market economy. After the decline of the Mughal Empire the eighteenth century saw the emergence of regional power centres which gave new impetus and direction to the already existing commercial patterns.

The vast econmic structure of the Mughal India was mainly based on agricultural production. The Mughal revenue policies were organized in such a way that it tended to generate a vast rural market. As the Mughals preferred to collect revenue in cash, a large part of agricultural produce had to be converted into money to pay taxes. Though, a majority of peasants cultivated coarse variety of crops, high value crops were also produced. All this entailed the marketing of cereals as well as cash crops. The peasants sold the part of their produce in the local markets but the share collected by the state as revenue in kind found its way to distant markets. The nomadic community of Banjaras played a pivotal role in the lifting of huge quantities of grain, salt and other necessities and subsequently in transporting the same to remote corners of the country. These Banjaras comprised Hindus, Muslims and Nanak Panthis as is evident from the sources and discussion in Chapter 1. They worshipped various folk deities, especially those; which they considered were possesing the healing and protective powers for them and their animals. Mainly the dieties worshipped by Banjaras were associated to the wellbeing of animals and most commonly to protect the bullocks from snake-bites. Culturally, the Banjaras were a distinct and cohesive community.

The organization of land transport was largely controlled by the Banjaras who lifted the grains from the surplus regions and transported it to the deficit areas. Thus, long-distance trade in bulk goods was carried out by Banjaras or nomads who lived with their families and animals in camps popularly known as *tandas*. The origin of the term is from the Marwari language, but a lot of places in Uttar Pradesh, Punjab, Maharashtra, Himachal Pradesh and Rajasthan are called *tandas*. All such places are located near some water body, and are on the routes. This is a clear indication that these zones were halting stations for the Banjaras while en-route due to availability of water and fodder. The nomenclature of the *tanda* villages indicates to the various popular *Naiks* (*tanda* leader) and the localities (distant places) from where the troops were arriving. Therefore, over the time, native people started refering these halting land segments as *tanda* area and even now in the twenty-first century these zones (halting) are known either, after the name of a *Naik* (*tanda* leader) or; the distantly located lands from where the *carvan* has arrived. The locals don't pay much attention to the fact that most of Banjaras are not inhabiting in these *tandas* now. The Banjara hills in Hyderabad accommodates the Banjara population who are now permanently settled there. A large *tanda* usually contained 600-700 persons or even 20,000 bullocks. They never lived in houses and they carried along with them their women and children. The chief as we know was called a *Nayak*. A single Banjara could possess as many as 100 oxen, sometimes even more. Demographically, they might have belonged to a fringe of vast continental society but their role as transporters and traders of food grain and other goods, made them indispensable as they were providers of the necessities for daily use. Chapter 2 firmly establishes the role of Banjaras as indispensable transporters, untill the introduction of Railways.

The Banjaras operated both as factors of wealthy merchants and individual traders. In both cases they sold their goods en-route and in remote markets. They traded in luxury as well as necessities. But much of their trade was in food grains, salt and other necessities, as has been discussed in Chapter 3. The commodities transported by the Banjaras clearly confirms that a large number of people depended for their supplies and survival on the arrival of the Banjara *carvans*. People in the deficit regions anxiously awaited the arrival of these *carvans* each year. All the evidences are clearly pointing to and establishing the economic and social significance of the Banjara as traders in medieval times.

As the Banjaras were a principal link for the supplies to the armies, they played a significant role in the outcome of prolonged campaigns. Their non-arrival in time could lead to military disasters for the depending army, as has been noted on certain occasions. Conversely, by supplying goods in time they could provide necessary boost to the rebellious elements such as the Sikhs during the siege of Sadhaura. Needless, to say that the Banjaras could play an indirect role in the outcome of military hostilities.

The nature of en-route conflicts between the nomadic Banjaras and the sedentrized peasants has been extensively discussed in Chapter 4. With the help of important archival sources we have been able to identify the various sources of tension between the Banjaras on the one side and peasants, local officials and petty-traders on the other. Apparently, the Banjaras instead of moving peacefully from place to place displayed a lot of aggressiveness towards other segments of society. Nevertheless their link with the sedentary society fluctuated between cordiality and conflict. Hence, the state did constantly kept watch of their movements and intervened swiftly to discipline them when the need arose and situation demanded negotiation and mediation.

It has been argued by Van Leur that peddling was the principle form of the 'traditional' Asian commerce.[1] At first sight the operations of the Banjaras might seem to be those of the 'peddlers'. However, no trace of communal possession of capital has been found among the Banjaras. The Banjaras owned cattle individually. Their coming together in large groups has led Tapan Raychaudhuri to say that 'here we have an instance of peddling trade organized on massive scale'.[2]

As not everyone could join a *tanda* freely and members were not free to carry whatever goods they wanted to take, the Banjaras trade can not be characterized as a peddling trade. As the Banjaras acted on behalf of rich merchants, their position as peddler becomes further untenable. In this work I have desisted from putting a label on the Banjaras' trade. However, the social significance of the Banjara trade has been highlighted by basing our argument on a variety of sources.

Chapter 5 provides an insight that, towards the end of the eighteenth century, the Banjaras began to lose their primacy as transporters of grain, salt, etc. With the establishment of railways in AD 1853 in India, the Banjara role as transporters came to a near close and they ceased to be nomadic and became sedentarized. An examination of colonial census reports reveals an almost imperceptible process towards the sedentarization of the Banjaras. The community was essentially wandering due to its professional requirement and this characteristic led them in a grapple with the tag of 'criminal' along with the another politicially crucial community of the eunuchs. Further, the criminalization of the community by the Company through the Criminal Tribes Act of 1871, ensured their elemination from the economic panorma of India. Though the Banjaras retained their tribal form, they were simultaneously being forced to reconstruct their social organization. This re-constructing was not entirely haphazard. Surely, the Banjaras had some well defined options open to them. Elsewhere in India they took to different occupations. But in the north-western regions, most of the Banjaras became cattle traders. Thus, buying and selling cattle in the annual fairs of Nagaur and Pushkar is their principal occupation today. Along with it the Banjaras also deal in herbs, which they proudly claim are collected by them while travelling. Though the variety of herbs are not specific to the area of the their trading but are rarities from the Himalayas and the Vindhaya forests. Many items of spiritual significance are also sold such as, *rudraksh*, pearls and large variety of gemstones, which they claim to have collected while roaming in the hilly and craggy areas.

Overall, it can be said with assertation that the Banjaras were traders and even today they try to associate with their past and historically respected profession, through which they attained the economic and social significance in the role of a trader. The nostalgic association of community with the past reflects the vaccum and the shaken economic and social condition of the Banjaras.

NOTES

1. Ashin Das Gupta, 'The Maritime Merchants, *c.* 1500-1800', Presidential Address Medieval India Section, *Proceedings of Indian History Congress,* 35th Session, 1974.
2. Tapan Raychaudhuri and Irfan Habib (eds.), *The Cambridge Economic History of India c. 1200-1750,* vol. I, Orient Longman in association with Cambridge University Press, New Delhi, 1982, p. 342.

APPENDICES

APPENDIX I

Banjara

NAZIR AKBARABADI

Tuk hirsh-o-hawa ko chor miya, mat desh-bidesh firai mara
Kazaak azal ka lutaai hai din-raat bajakar nakaara
Kya badiya, bhaisa, bail, shutur kya goonai palala sar bhara
Kya gehu, chawal, sotha, matar, kya aag, dhuwa kya angaara
Sab thaath pada raih jaa-waiga jab laad chalega banjaara. (1)

Gar tu hai lakhhi banjaara aur khaip bhi tairi bhaari hai
Ai gaafil ! tujh sai bhi chatur ek aur bada vyaapari hai
Kya shakar, mishri, kand, giri kya sambhar mitha-khaari hai
Kya dhaak, munakka, sonth, mirchi, kya kesar, long, supaari hai
Sab thaath pada raih jaa-waiga jab laad chalega banjaara. (2)

Tu badiya laadai bail bharai jo purab paschim jaa-waiga
Ya suud (suut) badhakar laawaiga ya tota ghaata paa-waiga?

Kajaak azal ka rastai mai jab bhaala maar giraa-waiga
Dhan-dulat, naati-poota kya ek kunba kaam na aa-waiga
Sab thaath pada raih jaa-waiga jab laad chalega banjaara. (3)

Har manzil mai ab saath tairai yai jitna daira danda hai
Zar daam-diram ka bhaanda hai, banduk sipar hai khaanda hai
Jab naayak tan ka nikal gaya jo mulko-mulko handa hai
Fir handa hai na bhaanda hai na halwa hai na maanda hai
Sab thaath pada raih jaa-waiga jab laad chalega banjaara. (4)

Jab chaltai-chaltai rastai mai yai goon tairi dhal jaa-waigi
Ek badiya tairi mitti par fir ghaas na charnai paa-waiga
Yeh khep jo tunai laadi hai sab hiso mai bat jaa-waigi
Dhi, puut, jamaai, beta kya, banjaaran pass na aa-waigi
Sab thaath pada raih jaa-waiga jab laad chalega banjaara. (5)

Kuch kaam nahi aa-waiga tairai yai laal-o-zumurd sem-o-zar
Jab punji baat mai bikhraigi har aan banaigi jaan uper
Nubat, nakaarai, baan, nishaa, dulat, hushmat, fujaai, lushkar
Kya masnad, takiya, mulk-makka, kya choki, kursi, takht, chatar
Sab thaath pada raih jaa-waiga jab laad chalega banjaara. (6)

Kyu jee par bojha uthaata hai een goono bhaari-bhaari kai
Jab moot lutaira aan pada fir dunai hai vyaapari kai

Kya saaj jadau, jar-jaiwar kya gootai than kinaari kai
Kya ghodai, jeen sunhairi kai kya haathi laal am-maari kai
Sab thaath pada raih jaa-waiga jab laad chalega banjaara. (7)

Mangrur na ho talwaaro par mat fool bharoosai dhaalo kai
Sab pata tod kai bhaagai-gai muh dekh azal kai bhaalo kai
Kya dibai moti hiro kai kya dhair khazaanai maalo kai
Kya bukchai taas tamaami kai kya takhtai shaal dushalo kai
Sab thaath pada raih jaa-waiga jab laad chalega banjaara. (8)

Kya shakhat makaa banaawat hai kham tairai tan ka hai poola
Tu uchai kot uthata hai va goor gadhai nai muh khola
Kya raini, khandak, rand badai, kya burj, kangura anmola
Ghad, kot, rahkala, toop, kila, kya sisa daru aur gola
Sab thaath pada raih jaa-waiga jab laad chalega banjaara. (9)

Har aan nafai aur totai mai kyu marta firta hai ban-ban
Tuk gaafil dil mai soch zara hai saath laga tairai dushman
Kya loundi, bandi, daai, dawa, kya banda, chaila naik chalan
Kya mandir, masjid, taal, kuwa kya khait baadi, fuul, chaman
Sab thaath pada raih jaa-waiga jab laad chalega banjaara. (10)

Jab marg fira kar chabuk ko yaih bail badan ka ha-kaiga
Koi taaz samaitaiga taira koi goon seir aur taakaiga
Ho dhair akaila jungal mai tu khaak lahaid ki faa-kaiga
Us jungal mai fir aah "nazir" ik bhunka aan na jhaa-kaiga
Sab thaath pada raih jaa-waiga jab laad chalega banjaara. (11)

बंजारा

टुक हिर्स-ओ-हवा की छोड़ मियां, मत देस-बिदेस फिरे मारा
क़ज़्ज़ाक़ अजल का लूटे है दिन-रात बजाकर नक़्क़ारा
क्या बधिया, भैंसा, बैल, सुतुर, क्या गौनें पल्ला सर भारा
क्या गेहूँ, चावल, सोठ, मटर, क्या आग, धुआं क्या अंगारा
सब ठाठ पड़ा रह जावेगा जब लाद चलेगा बंजारा (1)

गर तू है लक्खी बंजारा और खेप भी तेरी भारी है
ऐ ग़ाफ़िल! तुझसे भी चतुरा इक और बड़ा ब्योपारी है
क्या शक्कर, मिसरी, क़ंद, गरी क्या सांभर मीठा-खारी है
क्या दाख, मुनक़्क़ा, सोंठ, मिर्च, क्या केसर, लौंग, सुपारी है
सब ठाठ पड़ा रह जावेगा जब लाद चलेगा बंजारा (2)

तू बधिया लादे बैल भरे जो पूरब पच्छिम जावेगा
या सूद बढ़ाकर लावेगा या टोटा घाटा पावेगा?
क़ज़्ज़ाक़ अजल का रस्ते में जब भाला मार पावेगा
धन-दौलत, नाती-पोता क्या इक कुनबा काम न आवेगा
सब ठाठ पड़ा रह जावेगा जब लाद चलेगा बंजारा (3)

हर मंज़िल में अब साथ तेरे ये जितना डेरा डंडा है
ज़र दाम-दिरहम का भांडा है, बन्दूक़ सिपर है खांडा है
जब नायक तन का निकल गया जो मुल्कों-मुल्कों हाँडा है
फिर हाँडा है न भाँडा है न हलवा है न माँडा है
सब ठाठ पड़ा रह जावेगा जब लाद चलेगा बंजारा (4)

जब चलते-चलते रास्ते में यह ग़ौन तेरी ढल जावेगी
इक बधिया तेरी मिट्टी पर फिर घास न चरने पावेगा
यह खेप जो तूने लादी है सब हिस्सों में बंट जावेगी

धी, पूत, जमाई, बेटा क्या, बंजारन पास न आवेगी
सब ठाठ पड़ा रह जावेगा जब लाद चलेगा बंजारा (5)

कुछ काम न आवेगा तेरे यह लाल-ओ-ज़मुर्रद सीम-ओ-ज़र
जब पूंजी बात में बिखरेगी हर आन बनेगी जान ऊपर
नौबत, नक़्क़ारे, बान, निशां, दौलत, हशमत, फ़ौजें, लशकर
क्या मसनद, तकिया, मुल्क-मकां, क्या चौकी, कुर्सी, तख़्त, छतर
सब ठाठ पड़ा रह जावेगा जब लाद चलेगा बंजारा (6)

क्यों जी पर बोझ उठाता है इन ग़ौनों भारी-भारी के
जब मौत लुटेरा आन पड़ा फिर दूने हैं ब्योपारी के
क्या साज़ जड़ाऊ, ज़र-ज़ेवर क्या गोटे थान किनारी के
क्या घोड़े ज़ीन सुनहरी के क्या हाथी लाल अम्मारी के
सब ठाठ पड़ा रह जावेगा जब लाद चलेगा बंजारा (7)

मग़रूर न हो तलवारों पर मत फूल भरोसे ढालों के
सब पत्ता तोड़ के भागेंगे मुंह देख अजल के भालों के
क्या डिब्बे मोती हीरों के क्या ढेर ख़ज़ाने मालों के
क्या बुक़चे ताश, तमामी के, क्या तख्ते शाल-दोशालों के
सब ठाठ पड़ा रह जावेगा जब लाद चलेगा बंजारा (8)

क्या सख़्त मकां बनवाता है खम तेरे तन का है पोला
तू ऊंचे कोट उठाता है वां गोर गड़हे ने मुंह खोला
क्या रैनी, ख़दक, रंद बड़े, क्या बुर्ज, कंगूरा अनमोला
गढ, कोट, रहकला, तोप, किला, क्या शीसा दारू और गोला
सब ठाठ पड़ा रह जावेगा जब लाद चलेगा बंजारा (9)

हर आन नफ़े और टोटे में क्यों मरता-फिरता है बन-बन ?
टुक ग़ाफ़िल दिल में सोच ज़रा है साथ लगा तेरे दुश्मन

क्या लौंडी, बांदी, दाई, दवा, क्या बन्दा, चेला, नेक चलन
क्या मंदिर, मस्जिद, ताल, कुआं क्या खेतीबाड़ी, फूल, चमन
सब ठाठ पड़ा रह जावेगा जब लाद चलेगा बंजारा (10)

जब मर्ग फिराकर चाबुक को यह बैल बदन का हाँकेगा
कोई ताज समेटेगा तेरा कोई ग़ौन सिर और टाँकेगा
हो ढेर अकेला जंगल में तू ख़ाक लहद की फाँकेगा
उस जंगल में फिर आह 'नज़ीर' इक भुनका आन न झाँकेगा
सब ठाठ पड़ा रह जावेगा जब लाद चलेगा बंजारा (11)

Nazir Akbarabadi, the author of poem 'Banjara', was a poet of the nineteenth century. He was born in Delhi and had constant association with Agra. Kanwal (a Urdu Professor) compares Nazir Akbarabadi to Wordsworth as both were Romantic poets.[1] His poetry mainly highlights the difficulties faced and efforts made by the general public to acquire and arrange the basic day to day necessities of life like, food, cloth, etc. In the time-line of history he was based in the nineteenth century yet his poetry brings to light the difficulties of the twentieth century. The poetry reflects his far-sightness. That might have been the reason why he was never able to attain fame during his lifetime. As his poetry was not in tune with the contemporary times where much of Urdu poetry was about romance, spirituality, etc. But in the twentieth century he attained the title of '*Aawami Shayar*' and became immensely popular due to his solidarity with the social and economic issues and the constant struggle faced by human beings. Some of his famous poems are *Jawaani* (youth), *Aadmi-nama*, *Roti-nama*, *Chapatti-nama*, *Kodi-ki-philosophy* (philosophy of cowery – a substitute of money), *Rupai ki philosophy* (philosophy of currency note), *Budhapa* (old age), *Maut* (death) among many other brilliantly composed poems, highlighting the struggles of life. The poem is supplied here for the benefit of reader. A simple reading of poem is sufficient to get an insight in the dynamism of Banjara trader and the exhaustive list of items traded by them. A sense of *tanda* and its components also becomes visible.

NOTE

1. Ibn-i-Kanwal (ed.), *Nazir Akbarabaadi (ahwal-o-intakhaab)*, National Book Trust, Delhi, 2014.

APPENDIX II

The Instances of Conflicts Catalogued in *Arsatthas* Records

S. No.	*Nature of Conflict*	*Pargana*	*Amount of penalty in Rs., anna, paisa*	*Year in VS/AD*
1.	*Qanungo* made illegal extortion from the Banjara for which he was penalised.	Tonk	21	1768/1711
2.	Banjaras and *vacchaits* fought. The Banjaras were penalised.	Tonk	41	1768/1711
3.	Kesara Banjara was penalised for causing destruction in the standing crops.	Tonk	34	1768/1711
4.	Banjara destroyed the fields of Chaudhari Premaraj and Tara Chand. A penalty was taken from him.	Tonk	47	1768/1711

(Contd.)

APPENDIX II (Contd.)

5.	Sukha s/o Dhana took 21 bullocks and sold them to the Banjaras. From him fine was charged.	Tonk	9	1773/1716
6.	Banjaras were penalised for destroying the standing crop.	Tonk	5.8a	1774/1717
7.	Cotton was handed over to Banjaras against which an advance money was taken by the *patel.*	Tonk	27	1774/1717
8.	When the weighman of *qasba* weighed the rice brought by the Banjara, it was found less than the stated weight. The Banjara was penalised.	Dausa	10	1769/1712
9.	Banjara fought with the *sahna* (watch-man) for which the Banjara was penalised.	Dausa	1	1769/1712
10.	Banjara was penalised for destroying the fields of some unnamed peasant.	Dausa	3.12a	1769/1712
11.	Chittar Shah called the Banjaras and made illegal extortion from them. Due to this he was penalised.	Dausa	4	1769/1712
12.	Banjara was penalised for destroying the fields of the peasants. Penalty leived.	Dausa	3.12a	1769/1712
13.	Fight between *sahna* and Banjara. The Banjara was penalised.	Dausa	5	1769/1712

(Contd.)

APPENDIX II (Contd.)

14.	A *Khatik* (a menial caste) was penalised for stealing the bullocks of Banjara. *Thanedar* penalised the *Khatik*.	Dausa	50	1769/1712
15.	Banjara destroyed the standing crops for which he was penalised.	Dausa	3.12a	1769/1712
16.	Banjaras ruined the standing crops for which they were fined.	Dausa	5	1770/1713
17.	Banjaras causing destruction in the standing crops of village. Banjaras were charged penalty.	Dausa	5	1770/1713
18.	Banjara caused destruction of the village's standing crop for which a penalty was levied on the Banjara.	Dausa	10	1771/1714
19.	Banjara fed his bullocks in the standing crop for which a penalty was charged.	Dausa	1	1772/1715
20.	Bullocks of Banjaras ruined the crops of a village. The village officials caught them and took a penalty.	Dausa	1	1772/1715
21.	The mare of a Banjara strayed into the compound (*rama*) of a village. The mare was fed by the villagers who in return took money from the Banjara	Lalsot	2.8a	1774/1717
22.	Theft in Banjara camp. The thief was caught and penalised.	Lalsot	2.12a	1774/1717
23.	Bullocks of Haider Mani *Nayak* destroyed the fields for which he was penalised.	Lalsot	23	1794/1737

(Contd.)

APPENDIX II (Contd.)

24.	Sukhram Banjara's animals destroyed fields. He was penalised.	Lalsot	9	1794/1737
25.	Mahamani Meena's field was destroyed by the Banjaras who were fined.	Lalsot	1	1797/1740
26.	The Banjara destroyed the fields of an unnamed peasant for which a penalty was imposed.	Lalsot	2.8a	1797/1740
27.	When Gowardhan Banjara's bullocks destroyed the standing crop of *moth* (a pulse), he was penalised.	Lalsot	4a	1797/1740
28.	Bullocks belonging to the son of Jagannath Banjara destroyed the fields of cotton. Hence a penalty on him.	Malpura	3a	1793/1736
29.	Ramji *Nayak* Banjara's bullocks destroyed the standing crops of Girdha Jat. He was penalised.	Malpura	2a	1793/1736
30.	Chitar Banjara's bullocks spoiled the standing crop. A penalty was charged on him.	Malpura	2.1a	1799/1742
31.	Some unnamed Banjara caused destruction in the fields. He was penalised for the same.	Malpura	3	1799/1742
32.	Gidhwa Bohra had given some pots of *khand* (sugar) to a Banjara. While receiving them at qasba, two pots of sugar were found missing. A penalty was imposed on the Banjara.	Fagui	10	1778/1721

(Contd.)

APPENDIX II (Contd.)

33.	Banjara destroyed the crops by straying his bullocks into the field. A penalty was imposed and collected.	Fagui	5.2a	1778/1721
34.	A conflict between *vacchait* and Banjaras occurred when some goods out of the total were found missing. The Banjaras were penalised.	Fagui	10	1778/1721
35.	Banjara caused destruction in the field of Kirparam for this act Banjara was penalised.	Fagui	4	1790/1733
36.	Tension between *sahna* and Banjara. The Banjara entered the protected field of *sarkar* (government) for which he was fined.	Fagui	4.8a	1791/1734
37.	Tiff between the *sahna* and Banjara over the security of standing crops in which Banjara fed his cattle.	Fagui	8.2a	1791/1734
38.	Ram Singh Banjara caused destruction of the standing crops. He was penalised.	Bhartari	1	1722/1665
39.	Lakha *patel* sold dry grass to the Banjaras. The patel was fined as he was not supposed to do so.	Bhartari	2	1722/1665
40.	Ramdas Banjara ruined the standing crops of *moth* (a pulse). Hence a penalty was charged.	Bhartari	2	1722/1665
41.	Pema Ram Banjara spoiled the standing crop of *chana* (gram). He was penalised.	Bhartari	9	1722/1665

(Contd.)

APPENDIX II (Contd.)

42.	Nathu Banjara caused destruction in the fields. A penalty was charged.	Bhartari	3	1722/1665
43.	Girdha Banjara ruined the crops of *paagu* (oilseed). For this act he was penalised.	Bhartari	11	1722/1665
44.	Bahadur Banjara spoiled the crops. He was fined.	Bhartari	5	1722/1665
45.	Man Singh and Kerso Banjara caused destruction in the fields of peasants. They were fined.	Bhartari	9	1722/1665
46.	A *bheli* (heap) of *guwar* belonging to Jairam Patel was partially destroyed by the bullocks of Hirderam Banjara. The Banjara was penalised.	Chatsu	9.4a.1p	1722/1665
47.	When a Banjara was looted a penalty was imposed collectively on the qasba inhabitants.	Ao	25	1751/1694
48.	A Banjara was robbed of his belongings. The villages of *mauza* Mehrauli of *pargana* Ao were penalized by the local officials.	Ao	25	1751/1694
49.	A *tanda* of Banjaras was looted in the *mauza* Barwala. The villagers of the same village paid the penalty.	Ao	11	1751/1694
50.	When a Banjara fed his bullocks from the standing crops, he was penalised.	Pachewar**	1	1772/1715

(Contd.)

APPENDIX II (Contd.)

51.	When some Banjara fed their cattle in the collected grain, they were penalised.	Narayana	8	1781/1724
52.	When Kesar Banjara ruined the crops of sugarcane (*var*) field, he was fined and the amount of fine was collected on the spot.	Narayana	14	1781/1724
53.	Kayam Banjara ruined the crops of Sita Ram (a state official). For which the former was penalised.	Narayana	10	1791/1734

**Pachewar is a group of five *parganas* namely, Salawad, Gijgarh, Kuwawa, Mora etc., which were part of Jaipur state during the eighteenth century.

The information provided in this appendix has been taken from the *hasil-firohi* column of the *Arsatthas* of the respective *parganas* belonging to the Jaipur state. The *Arsatthas* provide comprehensive information about the total income and expenditure of the *pargana* of their origin. Basic data such as the total number of villages under sub-assignments and the Amber ruler's *khalisa* are given in them. The *Arsatthas* also gives the estimated income, arrears, returns and expenditure incurred under different heads in the pargana. The area under the *zabti* and *batai jinsi* crops for the entire *pargana* (and also separately for each village) is given in the *Arsatthas*. The amount of land revenue (*mal*) and the names and magnitude of numerous other cesses are also entered in them. They also provide abundant information about the society, sometimes even the seamy side of peasant life.

Despite some irritating gaps, they are a mine of information on the system of agricultural production, prices, and social tensions. Moreover, from the *hasil firohi* column of these *Arsatthas* we can not only construct a narrative of everyday form of peasant resistance but also get a graphic account of the nature and incidence of sundry other offences committed by the villagers.

APPENDIX III

Banjara ki Chhattri

WHILE TRAVELLING FOR a family wedding in the vicinity of district Sikar in Rajasthan, I and my elder brother (a dedicated history buff turned entrepreneur) got to locate this small monument which is locally famous as *'Banjara ki Chhattri'*.[1] Literally it means the canopy of Banjaras. It is an eighteenth century monument as per the dates inscribed in it. Exactly it is located in the *Kaharo ki dhaani*[2] in village/hamlet Goriya of tehsil Piprali at Sikar district.[3] Being an abandoned and unnoticed monument it neither attracts visitors nor is it lucky enough to warrant maintenance from the Archeological Survey of India (ASI). The monument caught our attention due to its architecture and the inscriptions recorded on ceiling, pillar, floor and the upper running shaft of the *chhattris.* The presence of dated inscriptions (VS 1844/AD 1787) made us alert to take a focused notice to it. The construction of *chhattris* is a rajput tradition, wherein the *chhattris* are made to commemorate the death of a rajput. Various *chhattris* find place in the records like Gaitore *chhattris* of the Kachhwaha kings of Amber-Jaipur kingdom.[4]

This is not the first monument to be known as a *Banjara ki Chhattri*. Various *chattris* are noticed and reported by the ASI with the same nomenclature '*Banjara ki Chhattri*' and have attained the status of a protected monument. Two *chhattris*[5] with the same nomenclature are mentioned in the Jaipur Circle of Archeological Survey of India.[6] One of these is also recorded by Indira Gandhi National Centre for the Arts and it is located in village Khandar of Sawai Madhopur district.[7]

The *chhattri* located in Lalsot has gained recognition and is mentioned in scholarly works.[8] The reporting of the sites at least ensures the future referencing wherein research can be conducted. Looking with great curiosity in the list of monuments acknowledged by the Jaipur circle of ASI, I was unable to find our monument in the list. Later a curious extension into the list of monuments from Sikar district was made. Further, it disheartened me as the only monument reported from Sikar is the Harsh-Harshanath temple.[9] It was built in AD 973 by a Shiva ascetic. The structure of this particular monument *Banjara ki Chhattri* (village Gouriya, *tehsil* Piprali, Sikar) is comparatively larger than the other Banjara *chhattris* which have been discussed earlier in the text (Sawai Madhopur and Lalsot) and complex too. As both the above discussed *chhattris* (Sawai Madhopur and Lalsot) are single canopy structures. The complete structure of this *Banjara ki Chhattri* (Gauriya, *tehsil* Piprali, Sikar) includes four *chhattris*[10] and two entrance doors with extended *chabutras*[11] (a raised platform for sitting); the western side entrance is broken, one small entrance,[12] one small building looking similar to the entrance arch, houses a room and marks the closed back side,[13] a semi-slab covered well with two staircases each with 11 steps[14] and a erected stand made of concrete for fixing of *chaak* (Persian wheel);[15] it is used to pull-up water with help of rope. The covering of wells with stone slabs and wooden planks is a common practice in semi-arid areas of Rajasthan. As water is a scarcity in these areas and the frequent sand storms are a very common peril. It is a mechanism to keep well-water safe from the sand which will make water non-potable. The steps of wells were mainly to reach the water which goes significantly low in summers, with the help of small utensils to save mixing of soil in water and use the scanty resource carefully. The west entrance is broken and only the base pillars are visible. The style of architecture is Indo-Islamic with onion shaped tops (domes) decorated with the line art which is one of the most popular and regular design for *chhattris*. The material used in construction is lime-mortar to fix the stones of irregular shapes which are available in abundance in the Aravalli ranges. It is a very common stone used in the areas around Sikar for construction purposes. As it was easily available in abundant quantity it didn't cause much financial strain either. Being a student of history I was trying to study the monument with diligence. Besides this the initiative which engaged me and motivated to write this piece of information were the inscriptions written,[16] inscribed[17] and painted[18] over the upper running shaft, ceiling, column, floor, pillar and shaft of the *chhattris* rspectively. The most interesting thing to note in the ceiling inscription is a human figure with a spear drawn by line art.[19] The four *chhattris* are on the four corners of the structure and each has a raised platform and eight pillars with concrete decorative hangings between pillars. The two entrances are rectangular in shape without the raised platform but with extended *chabutaras* on both sides which are covered with canopies.[20] The ceiling of *chhattris* which contains the line art drawing of a male Banjara with spear in hand contains 4 inscriptions (three of *dhundhari*[21] – nos. 1, 2, 3 and one in Urdu no. 4).[22] All the four inscriptions are single line inscription. Out of these 4 inscriptions two *dhundhari* inscriptions (nos. 1 & 2) are dated vikram samvat (vs) 1844/AD 1787.[23] Inscription no. 3 is not dated and no. 2 is dated as *Jaith Sudi* 3 vs 1844/AD 1787.[24]

The Urdu inscription is not dated and illegible. Some effort has been made to decipher it.[25] It might be irritating to read history through mathematical numbers but for better understanding and to keep confusion at bay the inscriptions have been numbered. Another Urdu inscription (no. 5) is noticed on the inner upper shaft of the *chhattri*.[26] Inscription (no. 6) is recorded on the floor of *chhattri* is inscribed in three lines.[27] It notes '*Kuwar Ji* (line 1) *Shree Maamji* (line 2) *Shree Kuwar Maam Singh* (line 3)'. Another inscription engraved on the floor is completely damaged (no. 7).[28] It is inscribed in 2 lines. Line one is completely damaged and from line 2 only four words can be identified (1. *Ku*, 2. either *cha* or *wa*, 3. *ba*, 4. *na*). The reading of it goes like this, either *Kucha Bana* (which is not giving any meaning to the site) and the other is *Kuwa* (well) *Ba-na* (these are initial letters of hindi *varnmala* for writing the word Banjara, as the inscription is not readable after these two letters). The later interpretation of inscription no. 7 helps to connect, might it was recorded to date the making of the well. As *Kuwa Bana* in *dhundhari* dialect means the well is made. Two more *dhundhari* inscriptions (nos. 8 and 9) are noticed on the upper column of the *chhattri.*[29] Both are single line inscriptions and are painted with *gairu* colour on the plastered cream colour upper (round) running column of the *chhattri*. Inscription no. 8 notes '*Shree Ramji Chattri Karigar Bheej*' and no. 9 goes like this '*Shree Mohan Lal Ji*'.[30] All these inscriptions are lying in a neglected state and are getting irreversibly damaged. Another inscription (no. 10) is inscribed on a grey sand stone pillar. It shows a wheel with 8 spokes.[31] Usually this type of wheel is used in the bullock-carts.

All the ten inscriptions (from no. 1 to 10) are not recorded. Therefore, considering it my duty towards the conservation of heritage I tried to photograph them. The quality of the pictures is not very good as it was an unplanned visit and not a field trip to the site of the monument. Thanks to my smart phone I could preserve a record however minor. Where in any further damage to the monument cannot be stopped with this academic activity. The least is that the present stage is recorded as it is; without any manipulation. The historical importance of the monument will only be recognized after conducting a fair research. The socio-economic and cultural significance of the monuments shall be fixed by a scholarly effort and insight. This reporting is an initial effort to bring the monument on record. Further, a look at the contemporary archival source material is essentially required to recognize and harness the social, cultural and economic significance of the monument and assess its importance for the natives in past and how the present populace associates with it.

NOTES

1. See Figures 1, 6, 7 and 14.
2. *Dhaani* is a Marwari word for a cluster of 5 to 10 houses. Usually these *dhaanis* house members of same clan. Such as in *Khara ki Dhaani*, all the houses will be of the kin and clan members of the Khara family only. Similarly *Mahariyo ki Dhaani* will only accommodate the Mahariya kins.
3. See www.onefivenine.com for map and location. Gouriya is surrounded by Sikar *tehsil* on western side, *tehsil* Nawalgarh on the north, *tehsil* Udaipurwati and *tehsil* Khandela on the Eastern side. It is 12 km away from headquarter Sikar and

115 kms from Jaipur. The *Kaharo ki Dhaani* is also listed in the PWD records of the district.

4. Manisha Choudhary, unpublished Ph.D thesis, 'The Political and Religious Dignitaries in the Court Protocol of the Jaipur State', submitted to Department of History, 2013, p. 255.
5. Namely these are called *Banjara ki Chhattri* and *Banjaro ki Chhatri* located at village Khandar of district Sawai Madhopur and village Lalsot of Dausa district (near Jaipur) respectively.
6. www.asijaipurcircle.nic.in/Lalsot-Banjaro%20ki%20 chhatri,html#pub.
7. www.ignca.nic.in/asp/all.asp?projectid=rjsmp2510001 and ignca.nic.in/asi_reports/rjsmp_251.pdf.
8. Chandramani Singh (ed.), *Protected Monuments of Rajasthan,* Jawahar Kala Kendra in collaboration with Publication Scheme, Jaipur, 2002, and R.C. Agrawala, 'Unpublished Railing Pillars from Rajasthan', *Lalit Kala*, no. 11, Bombay, 1962. Cf. www.asijaipurcircle.nic.in.
9. www.asijaipurcircle.nic.in/harsh-harshnath temple
10. See Figs. 1 and 14.
11. See Fig. 1 for broken entrance.
12. See Fig. 6.
13. Ibid.
14. See Fig. 8.
15. See Fig. 5.
16. See Figs. 3 (Inscription no. 5), 4, 10 (Inscription nos. 8 & 9).
17. See Figs. 2 (Inscription no. 10), 11 (Inscription no. 6), 9 (Inscription no. 7) and 12/13 (Inscription nos. 1, 2, 3 & 4).
18. See Fig. 10 (Inscription nos. 8 & 9). Both the inscriptions are painted in *gairu* (brick-red) colour.

19. See Figs. 12 and 13. In the centre a human figure is drawn with a spear in the hand. The drawing is in line art.
20. See Fig. 14.
21. The language used around the areas of Jaipur is called as *Dhundhari* after the nomenclature of region which is known as *Dhundhar* (an area of dearth and insufficient production). All the records of the Jaipur state are written in this language. The variety of the documents available in *Dhundhari* are preserved in huge quantity at Rajasthan State Archives in Bikaner.
22. See Figs. 12 and 13 and details provided at the base.
23. See Figs. 12 and 13.
24. See Fig. 13, upper inscription on the right side.
25. See details under Fig. 13 (Inscription no. 4).
26. See Figs. 3 & 4 (Inscription no. 5).
27. See Fig. 11 (Inscription no. 6)
28. See Fig. 9 (Inscription no. 7)
29. See Fig. 10 (Inscription nos. 8 & 9).
30. Ibid.
31. See Fig. 2 (Inscription no. 10)

BANJARA KI CHHATTRI: KAHARO KI DHAANI PIPRALI (*TEHSIL*), SIKAR (DISTRICT), RAJASTHAN

Figure 1: *Banjara ki Chhattri*, north-western side, the broken pillars are visible between the canopies in front. In the centre the well is located (photograph by the author).

Figure 2: Inscription no. 10: The wheel with eight spokes (photograph by the author).

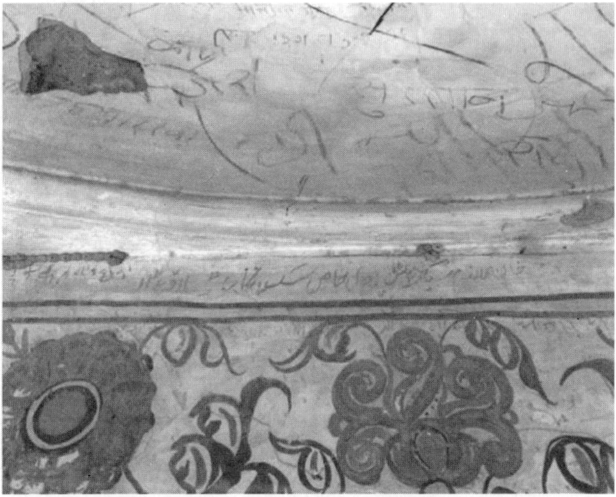

Figure 3: Inscription no. 5, one line Urdu inscription (photograph by the author).

Figure 4: Inscription no. 5, it records '*Khan mulazim-i-Sikar paltan awal khass Sikra Kanpur ilaka Badala*'. This specifies about the presence of Khan who is in service of Sikar's special contingent under Resident of Kanpur at Badala area. The date is missing. I owe special thanks to Prof. Farhat Hasan for helping me in reading this inscription (photograph by the author).

Figure 5: The structure for fixing of the *chaak* (Persian wheel) to pull-up water from well (photograph by the author).

Figure 6: *Banjara ki Chhattri:* The south-west side; a small entrance to the monument. The rectangle figure in the centre of the picture seen through the entrance in the background is the entrance to the small room made in the last section of the monument building. The room is facing north-west. Around it large open lands are available (photograph by the author).

Figure 7: *Banjara ki Chhattri:* The south-east entrance. The entrance on other side is broken (photograph by the author).

Figure 8: The well with a staircase. The identical-opposite side staircase is filled with garbage and the movement through the stairs is blocked (photograph by the author).

Figure 9: Inscription no. 7; the first line is illegible and in the second line only two letters are legible. Those are '*ku-wa-ba-na*' (photograph by the author).

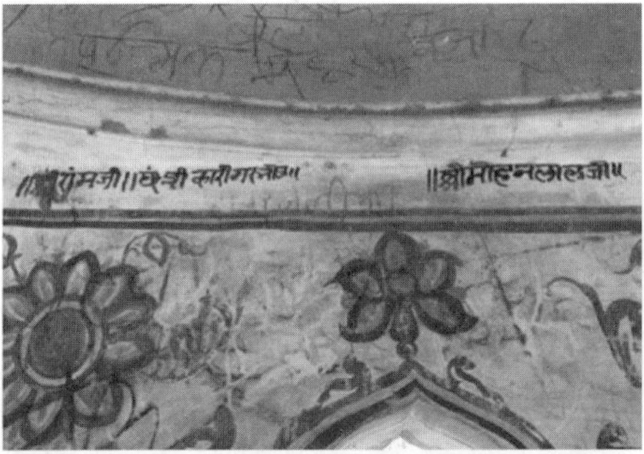

Figure 10: Inscription no. 8 is on the left side it says '*Shree Ramji, Chhattri Karigar Bheej*' and the right side noting is Inscription no. 9, the reading of it is '*Shree Mohan Lalji*' (photograph by the author).

Figure 11: It is Inscription no. 6 recorded in 3 lines. Reading of it is *Kuwarji* (line 1), *Shree Maam Ji* (line 2) and *Shree Kuwar Maam Singh* (line 3) (photograph by the author).

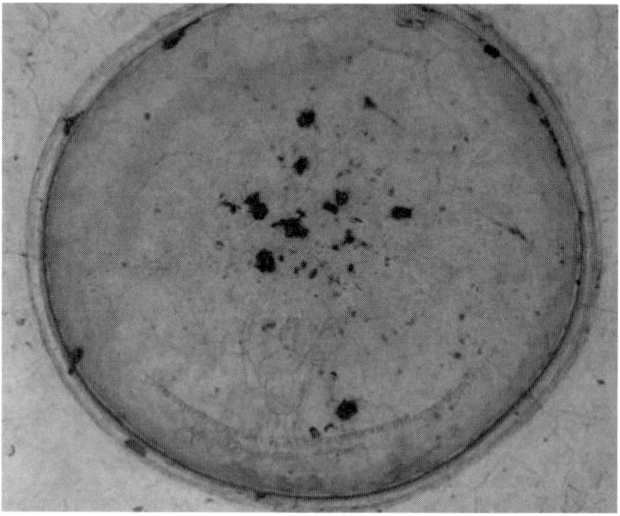

Figure 12: The ceiling of the *chhattri*. It contains the Inscription nos. 1, 2, 3 and 4. The line art draw depicting a Banjara male is in the centre of the inscriptions. Both inscriptions nos. 1 & 2 are dated VS 1844/AD 1787. Inscription no. 3 is in Hindi and Inscription no. 4 is written in chaste Urdu with a running *Shikasta* style by some well versed scribe accquinted with the free style writing of Urdu (photograph by the author).

Figure 13: Zoom in view of the ceiling depicted in Fig. 12 for better visibility of the inscriptions. Inscription no. 1 (on left side-upper line) is '*h. shoyanak raawalan narayanpur ka samvat 1844 ka*'. It means someone called Shoyanak Raawalan of Narayanpur has visited them at the *chhattri* in vs 1844/AD 1787.

Reading of Inscription no. 2 (on right side-upper line) is '*ram karanji saath aaya sikar gaya jaith sudi 3 samvat 1844 ka*'. This means a person named Ram Karanji came along with someone and went to Sikar. The date mentioned is *Jaith Sudi* 3, vs 1844/AD 1787.

Inscription no. 3 (on right side-lower line) state '*sovak saath hai ji*' which means sovak is with him or them. All the three inscriptions are in *Dhundhari*.

Inscription no. 4 (on left side-lower line) written in Urdu. It mentions '*Bhakar Mahal ka paas sarai Rohilla ka hissa pargana Rampur mauja Alwar.*' It notes about the location of a Bhakar Mahal which is located near sarai of Rohilla's in *pargana* Rampur of *mauja* Alwar.

All the three Hindi inscriptions (nos. 1, 2 & 3) are informative sentences in nature where the arrival, departure and accompany is mentioned. Reading of these inscriptions provides a sense that these notes were written as piece of information for someone who was expected to visit the *chhattri* for collecting the information about movement of the *tandas* (photograph by the author).

Figure 14: The main entrance with raised *chabutaras* on both the sides with small canopy covers. All the four *chhattris* on the four corners of the monument are visible and all are decorated with paint designs and is built-in lotus architectural style (photograph by the author).

Abbreviations

ASI	Archeological Survey of India
ASMI	*The Agrarian System of Mughal India*
IESHR	*The Indian Economic Social History Review*
IHR	*Indian Historical Review*
IN	Inscription
PIHC	*Proceedings of Indian History Congress*
RSAB	Rajasthan State Archives, Bikaner
SS	*Social Sciences*
SSP	*Social Sciences Probings*
VS	Vikram Samvat

Glossary

aakil	Bull
aawami shayar	People's poet
abadi	Habitation
amil	Collector of government revenue at the pargana level
amin	Revenue officer appointed in the pargana for assessment of revenue and local investigation
araj	Request or application
arsattha	A monthly treasury account of receipt and disbursement made up from daily entries
arzdasht	A written petition / letter addressed to the ruler
asami	Cultivator, revenue payer

asli	Original
Baldiya	Banjaras
baqaya	Previous dues
bichoti	Put up for sale
bigadu	Spoiler
bigha	Unit of area
bhomia	Local term for zamindar (holder of bhom)
bhailee	Collection or gathering
bohra	A moneylender
chitthi	Letter written by the diwan of Jaipur State to the pargana officials
charai	Grazing cess
chunda / chund	A ornament worn on head by married Banjara women
chuda	Bangle set
dakh	A spice
diwan	Chief minister of a state
du-fasli	Twice cropped land
dhundhari	A variant of the Rajasthan language spoken in the Jaipur region
dastur	Schedule of revenue rates
fasad	Riot
faujdar	Incharge of small army unit
giri	Almond

gunahgari	Penalty charged
gur	Jaggery
hasil	Actual realization of revenue
hasil ghas	Cess on grazing
hatti	Shop
hundi	Bill of exchange
huzure	Court of a ruler
ijafa	Increase
inam	Revenue free land grant
jawari	Millet
kapas	Cotton
karwanis	People of *carvan*
kasur	A fault
katra	Market
khand	Suger/jaggery sugar
khusamad	Appeasement
khechal / khinchal	Dispute
kirana	Food items
laata	Division
loun / lun	Salt
mahajan	A moneylender-cum-trader
manaba	To coax
mandi	Wholesale market
mauza	A village
mishri	Crystalized sugar

munakka	Big dry grapes / Raisins
mung	Green gram
munshi	A secretary to maintain accounts
nadari	Indigence
naj	Grains
nakal	Copy
paagu	A kind of oil seed
pargana	The administrative subdivision of a sarkar under the Mughals
patel	Headman of a village
patta	A deed of lease, a document given to a revenue payer, indicating his obligations
patwari	The village accountant
pout	Bales / bundles
Punya-udik	Charitable grant
qanungo	Hereditary revenue record keeper of a pargana
qasba	Town
rabi	Spring harvest
rahdari	Transit duties cess
raiyat	Peasant
rawla	Net amount
sarraf/sharoff/ shroff	Bullion merchant

sayana admi	Wise men
sahukar	Banker-cum-trader
sambhar	Salt
sarkar	Territorial subdivision of a province (*suba*) under the Mughals
sehna	Watchman
sehngi	Cess paid to the watchman
siro-pav	Robe of honour
sonth	A spice
supari	Areca-nut
syalu	Kharif
talluqa	Connection, a zamindari domain
tapppa	Subdivision of a pargana
taksirana	Penalty charges
ta'alluqa	A zamindari territory
tankhawah	Salary
tel	Oil
thanedar	Superintendent/in-charge
tulai	Cess for weighing grain
var	Mustard crop
vachhait	The one who works between the seller and buyer (broker).
vacchivittas	Foreign merchants
vyoparies	Trader
zabti	Method of land revenue assessment

	involving the measurement of land and payment of revenue in cash
zaraiti	Cultivated fields / crops
zortalab	Recalcitrant

Bibliography

ARCHIVAL SOURCES

I. *Arsatthas*

Arsatthas (mujmil), Pargana Tonk for the years VS 1768/AD 1711, 1773/ AD 1716, 1774/AD 1717, 1779/AD 1722.

Arsatthas (mujmil), Pargana Dausa for the years VS 1769/ AD 1712, 1770/AD 1713, 1772/AD 1715.

Arsatthas (mujmil), Pargana Lalsot for the years VS 1774/ AD 1717, 1794/AD 1737, 1797/AD 1740.

Arsatthas (mujmil), Pargana Bhartari for the years VS 1722/ AD 1665.

Arsatthas (mujmil), Pargana Chatsu for the years VS 1721/ AD 1664, 1772/AD 1715.

Arsatthas (mujmil), Pargna Malpura for the years VS 1719/ AD 1662, 1793/AD 1736, 1799/AD 1742.

Arsatthas (mujmil), Pargana Faguai for the years VS 1778/ AD 1721, 1790/AD 1733, 1791/AD 1734.

Arsatthas (mujmil), Pargana Ao for the years VS 1751/AD 1694.

Arsatthas (mujmil), Pargana Narayana for the years vs 1781/ AD 1724, 1791/AD 1734.
Arsatthas (mujmil), Pargana Gaywar for the year vs 1772/ AD 1715.

II. *Arzdashts*, from vs 1740/AD 1683 to vs 1766/AD 1709

III. *Amber Records*, from vs 1722/AD 1665 to vs 1724/ AD 1667.

IV. *Chitthiyat*

Chitthi to the *Amil* from Pargana Kotla, dated *Vaishak Sudi* 12, vs 1723/AD 1666.
Chitthi to the *Amil*, written by Vithal Das and Vijay Ram from Pargana Kotla dated *Mangsir Vadi* 12, vs 1723/AD 1666.
Chitti to the *Amil* written by Ajay Raj from Pargana Kotla, dated *Kati Vadi* 5, vs 1723/AD 1666.
Nakal Chitthi to the *Diwan*, written by Bohra Jagati Sur, dated *Asadh Sudi* 5, vs 1804/AD 1747.
Khat to Jait Singh Kamakar, Pargana Amber, dated *Fagun Sudi* 15, vs 1766/AD 1709.
Das, Shyamal, *Vir Vinod*, vols. 1-4, Motilal Banarsidass, Delhi, 1986.

Mughal Chronicles

Abul Fazal, *Akbar-nama*, tr. H. Beveridge, Low Price Publication, Delhi, 2011.
Badauni, Abdul Qadir *Muntakhab-ul Tawarikh*, 3 vols., tr. George S.A. Ranking, 1898, rpt. Idarah-i-Adabiyat-i Delhi, 1973.

Barani, Ziauddin *Tarikh-i-Firuz Shahi*, ed. Saiyid Ahmed Khan, Bibliotheca Indica, Calcutta, 1862.

Jahangir, *Tuzuk-i-Jahangiri*, ed. Syed Ahmad, Gazipur and Aligarh, tr. A. Rogers and H. Beveridge, 2 vols., London, 1909-14.

Nizamuddin Ahmad, *Tabaqat-i-Akbari*, vol. II, Calutta, 1931.

Gazetteer

Chopra, P.N., *The Gazetteer of India*, vol. II: *History and Culture*, Ministry of Information and Broadcasting, Govt. of India, Delhi, 6th edn., 2003.

Gahlot, Jagdish Singh, *Mardumshumari: Marwar Census Report: History of Western Rajasthans' Castes and their Rituals*, Research Centre, Jodhpur, 1891.

Jackson, William, 'A Lecture on Rail Roads, delivered on 12 January 1829: Before Massachusetts', Crockers and Brewster, Boston, 1829.

Powlett, P.W., *Gazetter of the Bikaner State*, Authority GOI, Calcutta, 1868.

Singh, Rai Bahadur Munshi Hardayal, *Report Mardumshumari: Marwar Census Report 1891*, Maharaja Man Singh Pustak Parkashan, Jodhpur, 2010.

Travel Accounts and Memoirs

Briggs, Captain, 'Account of the Origin, History and Manners of the Race of Men Called Bunjaras', Transactions of the Literary Society of Bombay, vol. I, London, 1819.

Buchanan, Francis, *A Journey from Madras Through the Countries of Mysore, Canara and Malabar*, vol. I, W. Bulmer and Co., London, 1807.

Crooke, William, *The North-Western Provinces of India: Their History, Ethnology and Administration*, Methuen & Co., London, 1897.

De Laet, *The Empire of the Great Mogol*, tr. John S. Hoyland, The British India Press, Mazgaon, Bombay, 1928.

Elliot, Henry M., *Memoirs on the History, Folk-lore and Distribution of the Races of the North Western Provinces of India*, vol. I, revised & rearranged ed. J. Beames, Trubner & Co., London, 1869.

Growse, F.S., *Mathura: A District Memoir*, Government Press, Allahabad, 1874.

Ibbetson, Denzil, *Punjab Castes*, The Superintendent, Government Printing, Punjab, Lahore, 1916; and B.R. Publishing Corporation, Delhi 1974.

Malcoln, John, *A Memoir of Central India including Malwa and Adjoining Provinces*, 2nd edn., Kingsburg, Paltbury & Allen, London, 1824.

Mundy, Peter, *The Travels of Peter Mundy in Europe and Asia 1608-1667*, vol. II: *Travels in Asia, 1628-1634*, ed. Lt. Col. Sir Richard Carnac Temple, Hakluyt Society, London, 1914.

Rose, H.A., *Glossary of the Tribes and Castes of the Punjab and North-West Frontier Province*, vol. II, Amar Parkashan, Delhi, 1980 (rpt.).

Russell, R.V. and Rai Bahadur Hira Lal, *The Tribes and Castes of the Central Provinces of India*, vol. II, MacMillan, London, 1916.

Sleeman, William, *Thugs and Phansigars of India*, Carey & Hart., Philadelphia, 1839.

Tavernier, Jean Baptist, *Travels in India*, tr. V. Ball and (revised by) W. Crooke, vol. I, MacMillan, London, 1889.

Tod, James, *Annals and Antiquities of Rajasthan or the Central and Western Rajpoot States of India*, vols. I-IV, Smith, Elder Co., rpt. Routledge Kegan Paul, London, 1957.

SECONDARY SOURCES

Alam, Muzaffar, 'Sikh Uprising under Banda Bahadur, 1708-1715', *Studies in History*, vol. I, no. 2, 1979, pp. 197-213.

Ali, Syed Aslam, 'The Role of Banjaras in Indian Trade During 17th Century', unpublished cyclostyled paper available in Aligarh Muslim University Library.

Bajekal, Madhavi, 'The State and the Rural Grain Market in Eighteenth Century Eastern Rajasthan', *The Indian Economic and Social History Review (IESHR),* New Delhi, 25 April 1988, pp. 444-74.

Bayly, C.A., *Rulers, Townsmen and Bazaars: North Indian Society in the Age of British Expansion c. 1770-1870*, Cambridge University Press, Cambridge, 1983.

Behal, Rana P. and Marcel van der Linden (eds.), *Coolies, Capital, and Colonialism: Studies in Indian Labour History*, International Review of Social History Supplements, Cambridge University Press, Cambridge, 2006.

Brennig, Joseph J., 'Textile Producers and Production in Late Seventeenth Century Coromandel', *IESHR*, vol. 23, no. 4, December 1986, p. 333-55.

Burman, J.J. Roy, *Ethnography of a Denotified Tribe: The Laman Banjara*, Mittal Publication, New Delhi, 2010.

Burn, Richard, *The Cambridge History of India*, vol. III, Cambridge University Press, 1934.

Chakravarti, Ranbir, *Trade and Traders in Early Indian Society*, Manohar, New Delhi, 2002.

Chandra, Satish, *History of Medieval India, c. 800-1700,* Orient Longman, New Delhi, 2007.

Choudhary, Manisha, 'Migrating Banjaras and Settling Tandas: An Un-noticed Contribution', *International Journal of History and Cultural Studies*, vol. 3, issue 4, 2017, pp. 26-35. A paper presented at International Seminar on Migration and Settlement: Development of Cross-Cultural India held at Jodhpur, 2017.

Choudhary, R.B.A., 'The Horse and Mughal Military Culture in Transition, 1526-1795', unpublished M.Phil. dissertation approved by Department of History, University of Delhi, 2014.

Chowdhury, Bhagirathi, 'Banjara', in *Encyclopaedic Profile of Indian Tribes*, ed. Sachchidananda and R.R. Parsad, Discovery Publishing House, New Delhi, 1996.

Deogaonkar, S.G. and Shailaja S. Deogaonkar, *Castes and Tribes of India: The Banjara*, vol. 3, Concept, New Delhi, 1992.

Devra, G.S.L., 'Sources on Trade and Trade-routes of Western Rajasthan (*c.* 1780-1848)', in *Sources of Socio-Economic History of Rajasthan and Malwa (1700 to 1900 AD)*, ed. N.S. Bhati, Maharaja Man Singh Pustak Parkashan, Jodhpur, 1989, pp. 52-7.

Eraly, Abraham, *The Mughal World: Life in India's Last Golden Age*, Penguin, New Delhi, 2007.

Frykenberg, Robert Eric, *Land Control and Social Structure in Indian History*, The University of Wisconsin Press, London, 1969.

Grover, B.R., 'An Integrated Pattern of Commercial Life in the Rural Society of North India during the Seventeenth and Eighteenth Centuries', in Sanjay Subrahmanyam (ed.),

Money and the Market in India c. 1100-1700, Oxford University Press, New Delhi, 1998, pp. 219-55.

Gupta, Ashin Das, *The World of the Indian Ocean Merchants c. 1500-1800,* compiled by Uma Das Gupta, Oxford University Press, New Delhi, 2004.

———, *Indian Merchants and the Decline of Surat, c. 1700-1750*, Manohar, New Delhi, 1994.

Gupta, B.L. *Trade and Commerce in Rajasthan during the 18th Century*, Jaipur Publishing House, Jaipur, 1987.

Gupta, S.P., *The Agrarian System of Eastern Rajasthan c. 1650-1750,* Manohar, New Delhi, 1986.

Habib, Irfan, *The Agrarian System of Mughal India c. 1556-1707,* 2nd revd. edn., Oxford University Press, New Delhi, 1999.

———, 'Merchant Communities in Pre-Colonial India', in James D. Tracy (ed.), *The Rise of Merchant Empire c. 1350-1750,* Cambridge University Press, Cambridge, 1990.

———,'Usuary in Medieval India', *Comparative Studies in Society and History*, vol. 6, no. 4 (July 1964), pp. 393-419.

———, 'Economic History of Delhi Sultanate: An Essay in Re-interpretation', *Indian Historical Review*, 4, 1977, pp. 92-103.

_____, *An Atlas of the Mughal Empire,* Oxford University Press, New Delhi, 1982.

Haider, Najaf, 'The Quantity of Theory and Mughal Monetary History', *The Medieval History Journal*, 2, 1999, pp. 309-48.

Hasan, S. Nurul, 'Zamindars under the Mughals', in Robert Eric Frykenberg (ed.), *Land Control and Social Structure in Indian History*, The University of Wisconsin Press, London, 1969 and 1st revised Indian edn., Manohar, New Delhi, 1979, pp. 17-32.

Hasan, S. Nurul and S.P. Gupta; 'Price of Food Grains in the

Territories of Amber (*c.* 1650-1750),' *Proceedings of Indian History Congress,* 29th session, Patiala, 1967, pp. 345-67.

Irvin, William, *The Army of the Indian Mughals: Its Organisation and Administration,* Low Price Publication, Delhi, rpt. 2004.

Jafri, S.Z.H, *Awadh from Mughal to Colonial Rule: Studies in the Anatomy of a Transformation,* Gyan Publishing House, New Delhi, 2016 (rpt.).

Kapur, Nandini Sinha, *State Formation in Rajasthan: Mewar During the Seventh-Fifteenth Centuries,* Manohar, New Delhi, 2002.

Kasturi, Malavika, *Embattled Identities: Rajput Lineages and the Colonial State in Nineteenth Century North India*, Oxford University Press, New Delhi, 2002.

Kennedy, M., *The Criminal Classes in India*, Mittal Publications, Delhi, 1985.

Khan, Dominique-Sila, *Conversion and Shifting Identities: Ramdev Pir and Ismailis in Rajasthan*, Manohar, New Delhi, 2003.

Khan, Kanwar Ali, *The Kachhwahas under Akbar and Jahangir*, Kitab Publishing House, Delhi, 1971.

Kolf, Dirk H.A., *Naukar, Rajput and Sepoy: The Ethnohistory of Military Labour Market in Hindustan, c. 1450-1850*, Cambridge University Press, Cambridge, 1990.

Kumar, Ram Krishan, 'Internal Trade System in Eastern Rajasthan (1720-1780)', unpublished Ph.D. thesis approved by Department of History, University of Delhi, 2006.

Levi, Scott Cameron, 'The Banjara: Medieval Indian Peddlerss and Military Commissariat', unpublished dissertation at University of Wisconsin, Madison, 1994.

Marshall, P.J. (ed.), *The Eighteenth Century in Indian History*,

Oxford University Press, New Delhi, 5th impression, 2011.

Moosvi, Shireen, *People, Taxation, and Trade in Mughal India*, Oxford University Press, New Delhi, 2008.

Mukhia, Harbans, 'Illegal Extortions from Peasants, Artisans and Menials in Eighteenth Century Eastern Rajasthan', *IESHR*, vol. XIV.2, 1977, pp. 231-45.

Narayan, Jagat, *Ajmer and Mughal Emperors*, Neha Vikas Prakashan, Kota, 1997.

Om Prakash, 'On Coinage in Mughal India', *Indian Economic Social History Review*, 25:4. 1988, New Delhi, pp. 475-91.

Prasad, Beni, *History of Jahangir*, Indian Press, Allahabad, 1940.

Rana, R.P., *Rebels to Rulers: The Rise of Jat Power in Medieval India*, New Delhi, Manohar, 2006.

———, 'Agrarian Revolts in Northern India during the Late 17th and Early 18th Centuries, *IESHR*, vol. 18, nos. 3 & 4, 1981, pp. 287-326.

———, 'A Dominant Class in Upheaval: The Zamindar of a North Indian Region in the Late Seventeenth and Early Eighteenth Centuries', *IESHR*, vol. 24: 4, 1987, pp. 395-410.

———, 'Everyday Forms of Peasant Resistance in Eastern Rajasthan (*c.*1660-1750)', *Social Science Probings*, vol. 15, nos. 3-4, 2003, pp. 41-62.

Ratnawat, Shyam Singh and Krishna Gopal Sharma, *History and Culture of Rajasthan from Earliest Time upto 1956 AD*, Centre for Rajasthan Studies, University of Rajasthan, Jaipur, 1999.

Raychaudhuri, Tapan, 'The Agrarian System of Mughal India', *Enquiry*, N.S., vol. 2: 1, 1965, pp. 92-121.

Raychaudhuri, Tapan and Irfan Habib (eds.), *The Cambridge*

Economic History of India c. 1200-1750, vol. I, Orient Longman in association with Cambridge University Press, New Delhi, 1982.

Rizvi, S.A.A., *The Wonder That Was India c. 1200-1700*, vol. II, Rupa and Co., Delhi, 1993; Picador India, London, 2005.

Sachchidananda and R.R. Parsad (eds.), *Encyclopaedic Profile of Indian Tribes*, vol. I (A-E), Discovery Publishing House, New Delhi, 1996.

Sahu, C., *Encyclopaedia of Indian Tribes*, Sarup and Sons, New Delhi, 2000.

Sato, Masanori and B.L. Bhadani, 'The Economy and Polity of Rajasthan: Study of Kota and Marwar (17th-19th Centuries)', Publication Scheme, Jaipur, 1997.

Sharma, G.N., *Social Life in Medieval Rajasthan (1500-1800): With Special Reference to the Impact of Mughal Influence*, Lakshmi Narain Agarwal, Agra, 1968.

Sharma, Shree Ram, *Banjara Samaj*, Dakshin Parkashan, Hyderabad.

Singh, Chetan, 'Conformity and Conflict: Tribes and the "Agrarian System" of Mughal India', *IESHR*, vol. 25, no. 3, 1988, pp. 319-40.

Singh, Dilbagh, 'Role of Mahajans in the Rural Econmy of Eastern Rajasthan During the Eighteenth Century', *Social Scientist*, vol. 2 (55), 1974, pp. 20-31.

———, 'Caste and Structure of Village Society in Eastern Rajasthan During the Eighteenth Century', *Indian Historical Review (IHR)*, vol. 2, 1976, pp. 299-331.

———, *The State Landlords and Peasants: Rajasthan in the Eighteenth Century*, Manohar, New Delhi, 1990.

Singh, N.P., 'The Deplorable Condition of Saltpetre Manufacturers of Bihar, 1773-1833', in *Essays in Modern*

Indian Economic History, ed. Sabyasachi Bhattacharya, Munshiram Manoharlal, New Delhi, 1987, pp. 102-7.

Sinha, Nitin, *Communication and Colonialism in Eastern India: Bihar, 1760's-1880's*, Anthem Press, London and New York, 2012.

———, 'Mobility, Control and Criminality in Early Colonial India, 1760's-1850s', *IESHR*, vol. 45, January 2008, pp. 1-33.

Smith, John D., *The Epic of Pabuji: A Study of Transcription and Translation*, Katha Books, New Delhi, 1991.

Smith, W.C., 'Lower Class Uprising in the Mughal Empire', *Islamic Culture*, vol. 10, 1946, pp. 21-40.

Stein, Burton, *A History of India*, Oxford University Press, New Delhi, 2009.

Stokes, Eric, *Peasants and the Raj: Studies in Agrarian Society and Peasant Rebellion in Colonial India*, S. Chand & Co., Delhi, 1978.

Thapar, Romila, 'The Scope and Significance of Regional History', Presidential Address to the Punjab History Conference, Patiala, 1976.

Tracy, James D. (ed.), *The Rise of Merchant Empires: Long Distance Trade in Early Modern World c. 1350-1750*, Cambridge University Press, Cambridge, 1990.

Trembath, Shirley, 'The Rani Bhatiyani Songs: New or Recycled Material', in N. Singhi and Rajender Joshi (ed.), *Religion, Rituals and Royalty*, Rawat Publication, Jaipur, 1999.

Vardy, R.G., 'North Indian Banjaras: Their Evolution as Transporters', *South Asia Journal of South Asian Studies*, 1979, pp. 1-18.

Verma, H.C., *Medieval Routes to India: Baghdad to Delhi: A Study of Trade and Military Routes*, Naya Parkash, Calcutta, 1978.

Wills, C.V., *A Report on the Land Tenures and Special Powers of Certain Thikanedars of the Jaipur State*, The Jaipur Gazette, Jaipur, 1935.

Ziegler, Norman P., 'Rajput Loyalities During the Mughal Period', in J.F. Richards (ed.), *Kingship and Authority in South Asia*, Oxford University Press, New Delhi, 1978, pp. 242-84.

———, 'The Marwari Historical Chronicles: Sources for the Social and Cultural History of Rajasthan', *IESHR*, 13 (2), 1976, pp. 219-50.

LITERATURE

Akbarabadi, Nazir, 'Banjara Nama' (Poem), *Intikhab-i-Nazir Akbarabadi*, Delhi, Maktaba Jamia, 1970.

Ibn-i-Kanwal, *Nazir Akbarabadi (Ahwal-o-Intakhab)*, collection of poems, National Book Trust, New Delhi, 2014.

INTERVIEW/INTERACTIONS

Personal interview with Banjaras, who were camped at Sikar district during the month of May, July, October and December 2008 and January 2015. The interaction was with whole community while their Panchayat was in session.

ONLINE ACCESS

- Railways Regulation Act, 1840. online access www.legislation.gov.U.K.
- Railways Regulation Act, 1844. online access www.legislation.gov.U.K.
- www.irfca.org.

Index

Plate 1: A Lohar woman (photograph by the author).

Plate 2: The *Gaada* is visible behind the mud wall studded with copper flower motifs (photograph by the author).

Plate 3: A Banjara couple and the make-shift house in the background (photograph by the author).

Plate 4: The members of *tanda* (photograph by the author).

Plate 5: A Lohar woman working on iron-tools (photograph by the author).

Plate 6: A *Gogaji* temple in *tanda* with a flag of Baba Ramdev sect (photograph by the author).

Plate 10: The step-wise tent settlements in a *tanda* (photograph by the author).

Plate 11: An elderly Banjara *Nayak*, wearing earrings made of gold (photograph by the author).

Plate 12: Canarians bringing wheat on oxen packs to Goa from Balaghat for selling. The load hanging on both sides of ox in bales is 'double-loading technique' (Facsimile XXXIV, *Imagens do Oriente*).

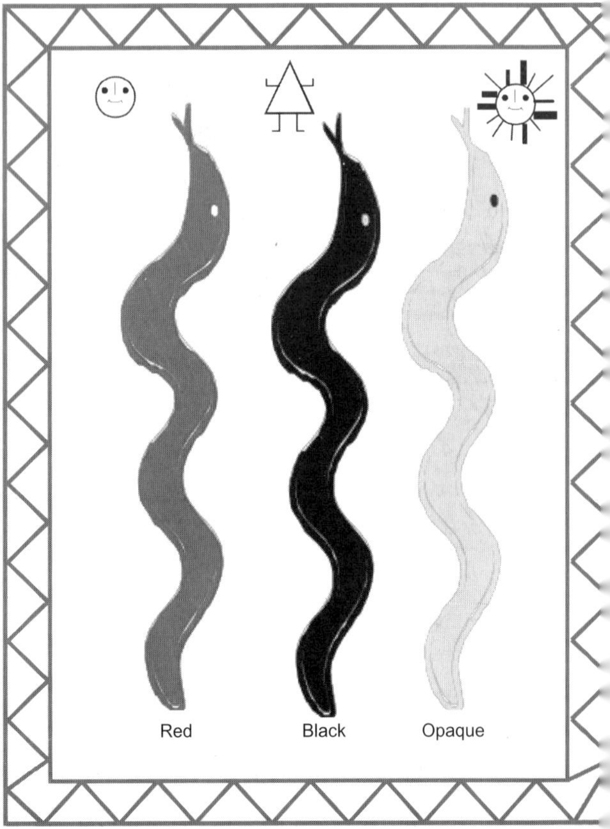

Plate 13: A drawing on the wall for worship of *Gogaji* (draw
by the author).